MW01073580

A SHORT GUIDE TO

WOMEN'S
MINISTRY

A SHORT GUIDE TO WOMEN'S MINISTRY

Nora Allison

PUBLISHING
BRENTWOOD, TENNESSEE

Published by B&H Publishing Group
Brentwood, Tennessee

Dewey Decimal Classification: 248.843
Subject Heading: WOMEN \ CHRISTIAN LIFE \ DISCIPLESHIP

Cover design by B&H Publishing Group.
Illustration by The Autumn Rabbit Ltd/Creative Market.
Author photo by Mary Chris Lajom.

1 2 3 4 5 6 • 27 26 25 24

Dedication

For my incredible kids, Lauren, Hanell, and Luke, and their spouses, Troy, Mike, and Chelsi.

In unique and sacrificial ways, you use your time, gifts, means, and abilities to help many others grow to know God, become more like him, and spread his fame. My picture of God continues to expand as I see his image clearly displayed in each of you. I couldn't be prouder or love you more!

Appreciation

HEART-FELT THANKS TO MY sweet friend, Terri Derhake, who read each word of my draft and encouraged me every step of the way. Your thoughtful, kind, positive input is appreciated more than you will know!

A huge thank you to my editor, Mary Wiley, for taking a chance on this first-time author and making my writing process a joy.

Eternal thanks to Lana Wolfe, who first shared the truth of Christ with me, to Pastor Bruce Boria, who trusted me to shepherd women, and to all those who used their gifts to help me grow to know God, become more like him, and spread his fame.

An extra special thank you to my husband and best friend, Gregg, whose belief in me, which often surpasses my own, enabled me to put my thoughts and experiences into writing. Without your urging, this book would not have happened and your feedback throughout was invaluable. I love you now and will forever.

Contents

Introduction

I CAN'T EVEN TELL you how very happy and humbled I am that you picked up this book and plan to read it. I've been a director of women's ministry in two different local churches for more than fifteen years, during which time I have eagerly "authored" many courses, classes, events, and programs to help women grow to know God better, and to step into opportunities to teach and lead and serve others. The idea of authoring a book, however, was not on my radar until various church leaders, including my husband, urged me to take what was happening with the women at our church and make the "whats" and "hows" and "whys" available to others. Once all the excuses I had for not writing ran out, I sat down at my computer and you're now holding the result.

The questions I get asked most often by interested folks is how I went about developing ministries to women "from scratch." How did I start? How did I decide what to do? How did I help grow leaders? What worked and what didn't? And of course, can you share your ideas with me?

The answers to these—and other questions—I've put in this book.

Honestly, I'd much rather be learning, explaining, teaching, showing, and doing ministry *with* you than typing out a manuscript. I wish I could know you, your heart, your challenges, and the particulars of your situation. Time and space limitations make that impossible, but I sincerely hope you will sit down with me through these pages and in some way identify with the opportunities, questions, issues, and needs that I faced and then be helped by how God led me through them.

It became my passion and purpose early on as a women's ministry director to provide the women I served with all the teaching, training, and leadership opportunities possible for them to flourish and the whole body of Christ to be built up. In too many of our churches, the desire is present for all to grow and use their gifts, but actual discipleship of the women is neglected. A church's sound theology is essential, but if unaccompanied by an equally robust practice, it can become a frustrating place where people are inadvertently overlooked, and growth is stunted. Sidelining women is rarely, if ever, the intent, but when leadership training and opportunities are inadequate or even absent for half the church, marginalization is the real-world result and then the whole church suffers. The Holy Spirit couldn't have been clearer that women and men alike are to be shepherded into complete "adulthood" in Christ: "We proclaim him, warning and teaching *everyone* with all wisdom, so that we may present everyone mature in Christ" (Col. 1:28, emphasis added).

So how do we do that? How do we help women at every stage of life and spiritual maturity grow to know God, understand and apply the gospel in their everyday lives, walk moment by moment with God's Spirit, and develop and use their talents and gifts? How do we play a part in shaping the hearts of women into Christlike hearts? And as we discover developing "stars" in God's kingdom, how do we employ God's means to nurture and "polish" them for his glory?

Millions of words have been penned on various aspects of this. My goal in this book is to put at your fingertips as many foundational principles and practical plans—grounded in biblical truth—as I can, so that whether you're in a leadership role at your church or hoping to impact a few friends or neighbors, you will find something helpful here.

One lesson you'll see as you go through the pages that follow is that we all learn as we go. I never had a grand plan of exactly what the final product would look like, what ministries we would end up with, or precisely how to get there. Needs were discerned, decisions were made, and plans developed as God revealed them. Ministry, like life, is made up of hope-filled daily choices and tasks, bathed in prayer, and then chock-full of edits to our best-laid plans.

A principle for all we do, of course, is to keep the goal in mind. We may never have a clear picture of exactly what the fruit of our labors will look like, but we know that hearts and lives shaped by the gospel and image-bearers transformed into God's true doppelgangers is a goal for each of us!

I pray this book serves as a resource, providing you with ideas for discipling women into maturity in Christ. Some of these resources you may be able to adopt as is, while others you will need to adapt to your context. Still other concepts may not be for you at all but instead will spur on your creativity to something much better for the women you care about.

So, as I write, I'm praying for you, that God will use what he has inspired (and blinds you to what is not from him) so that you and all those in your sphere of influence may grow and that, as a result, all in his kingdom will flourish.

CHAPTER 1

A View of Women: Aristotle vs. God

BORN IN 384 BC, Aristotle, renowned philosopher and scientist, is heralded as one of the greatest intellectual figures in all of Western history. Here are some things he had to say about women:

- Males have more teeth than females in the case of men, sheep, goats, and swine.
- Whoever is not like his parents is in some way a monster because nature has in these cases wandered in some way from the essential character. The first beginning of this is when a female was born instead of a male.
- The female is, as it were, a mutilated male.

- Females are weaker and colder in nature, and we must look upon the female character as being a sort of natural deficiency.[1]

God (and this tooth-deficient, mutilated, monstrous author) begs to differ. From the very beginning, God tells us that women and men alike are his handiwork. His masterpieces. His magnum opus. After creating the world and everything in it, he saved the best for last: humanity in two, beautiful, complementary forms bearing the very image of God.

> God created man in his own image;
> he created him in the image of God;
> he created them male and female. (Gen. 1:27)

Following their creation, God assigned to both men and women the esteemed task of ruling over the earth and filling it with their offspring in a paradisaical setting. When their selfish desires took precedent over God's, however, they intentionally defied his ordained instructions. The rest, as they say, is history. And although men and women alike, from that time on, would often prove to be deficient and even monstrous, they still bear his image, they need each other, and they are both essential in the flourishing of God's church.

This may be an obvious truth statement to some, but many women have, for too long, experienced neglect in their local churches. Church leaders frequently design their programs to teach, train, and disciple men, but what is often sadly lacking is a strategic vision and plan to develop women. Although a grievous omission, this is rarely an intentional shunning. It's usually merely oversight or is based on false assumptions about what women want and need. The singular focus on men is not meant to harm or hold women back. Nonetheless, it does just that. However unintentional and benign the aim, it's still neglect. And this neglect does serious harm to women and to the entire church.

Furthermore, many women in our churches do not seek growth opportunities. They self-limit, having inherited a very restricted view of what Christian women can and should do. Historical beliefs, after the pattern of Aristotle, that women are inferior and ought only to do as they are told, have carried over into some women's thinking today. They hold back their voices and forego using their gifts for fear that they will be judged "pushy" or unfeminine. They have no expectation that their gifts will be developed and used within the body. The mature Christian woman, they've understood, is compliant and passive. For years, I accepted the unbiblical (although perhaps culturally accurate) notion that the church and, by way of inference, God, expected less of me because I was female. The "heavy lifting" theologically was assigned to godly males, while my primary focus was to gently support the men. I wasn't basing my judgment on gifting, ability, preference, or position of authority, but solely on gender. It was only as I immersed myself in Scripture and was encouraged by my theologian husband that I began to see God's vision for all his image-bearers.

God, in his Word, instructs all believers to know him intimately and deeply. Each one is commanded to seek his wisdom and walk in his ways (Ps. 1). The Son of God encouraged men *and women* to learn from him and to follow him. Women were warmly included in Jesus's larger circle of followers (Luke 8:1–3). And just prior to his ascension, Jesus directed his closest disciples to make more disciples in and of all the nations, no gender specified (Matt. 28:18–20).

Why must we teach, train, and disciple women? Because it is God's desire and design. Because it is modeled beautifully by Jesus. And because God's image is best reflected by all his image-bearers as they grow to be more like him.

God makes his will for women clear in his Word:

- God created men *and women* to be co-reflectors of his image (Gen. 1:26–28). In God's plan, he made each one of us to resemble and reflect him and for women and men together to multiply his image-bearers.

- God ordained that men *and women* co-rule his creation (Gen. 1:28). Women and men together are to cultivate, domesticate, and take responsibility for the world around us.

- God appointed men *and women* alike to be coheirs of the grace of life (1 Pet. 3:7). Equal honor is to be given to women and men as they equally share in an inheritance from God and will stand together around his throne.

- God called men *and women* alike to give blessings and to inherit a blessing (1 Pet. 3:9). Women and men are summoned to unity, love, compassion, and humility for the good of all.

- God gives gifts to men *and women* alike for everyone's benefit, just as he desires (1 Cor. 12:4–26). There are no gender-specific gifts given for the growth of the church; rather, all women and men, and their contributions, are necessary and are to be developed and enjoyed.

- God recorded for all time the stories of men *and women* alike whose faith was exemplary (Heb. 11). Women and men are commended for demonstrating trust in God and his ways through faith-defying circumstances.

- God gave to an elderly woman the privilege of being the first human to prophesy aloud that Jesus is the Messiah (Luke 1:42–45). God reveals himself to women and men and encourages both genders to spread his fame.

- God incarnate, born of a woman, included numerous women in his band of disciples (Luke 8:1–3; 10:38–42; 7:36–50; John 20:11–18). He praised them for their desire to learn from him and for their worship of him, and he appeared first to them after his resurrection.
- God assigned women the task of encouraging and training other women in the distinct responsibilities afforded them (Titus 2:3–5). Mature women are to be models in their speech and behavior, teaching younger women how to be godly wives and mothers.
- God decreed that men *and women* alike are indispensable in the building up of Christ's church (Eph. 4:15–16). Women and men play essential roles in bringing all believers to maturity.

Taking a closer look at Ephesians 4:15–16, we read:

> Speaking the truth in love, let us grow in every way into him who is the head—Christ. From him the whole body, fitted and knit together by *every supporting ligament*, promotes the growth of the body for building itself up in love *by the proper working of each individual part.* (emphasis added)

For women the task is clear. We are to learn and change and grow up into Christ, properly doing our "individual part," not for our own benefit (although we will benefit!), but so the whole church is built up and so the whole church becomes more Christlike. We contribute to building the church by growing into maturity ourselves and by carrying out the essential role each of us was given to play in helping others do the same.

Whether or not we hold a formal position in the church, women are vital to its growth because the whole church depends on "*every* supporting ligament" properly working. For that to happen, all women must be students of God and of his Word. We need to know the truth about God and have an accurate picture of who God made us to be. We must be shown all that is ours as Christ-followers, trained in discerning and meeting needs, taught how to lead and teach others, and instructed in practicing the spiritual disciplines. We need to be given opportunities to use our gifts, encouraged with ways to improve, and then provided with additional opportunities. We need to know that we have an essential function in the church, and we need advocates so that others know that too.

We must disciple women because, as we've seen, women in all stages and walks of life are called to:

- accurately reflect God's image
- take responsibility to care for and influence the world in which we live for God's glory
- fully experience and rejoice in our inheritance of the grace of life
- be a blessing and enjoy our God-given blessings
- identify our gifts, develop them, and have opportunities to put them into practice

- grow in our trust in God and act on that trust, even in the most difficult of circumstances
- encourage and train other women and be encouraged and trained by them
- recognize God at work and spread his fame
- live out our God-given femaleness with strength, wisdom, and dignity, and do our part to build up God's church to full maturity

We disciple women because Jesus did. And we disciple women because women have something to teach us about who God is that men can't (and vice versa). Abigail Dodds gets it right. She writes:

> Aren't we thankful that God is more pow-erfully represented by uniting diversity to the praise of his glory? So it is with male and female. His revelation to us is that he is reflected by both. He gets more praise when women and men praise him. Man and

woman are his image. But as women, we have the privilege of fully expressing our part. Without our full expression of it, we rob God of his full glory. . . . We [women] tell a story with all we say and do about who God is. That God made you a woman is an essential part of the story he is telling about himself.[2]

As the director of ministries to women for many years, I was privileged to have worked with male leaders who either encouraged me profusely or so thoroughly ignored me that in both cases, I was able to thrive in developing ministries to women. I had maximum freedom to train women to shepherd other women and to use their God-given gifts. I could focus and God led me to many outstanding women to focus on! I discovered scores of capable women who helped start Bible studies, trained others in doctrine, schooled women in Christian beliefs and practices, led and multiplied mentor groups, raised up teachers, and created an atmosphere of fellowship and hospitality for all. They could brainstorm and plan and knew that their contribution mattered. In short order, women's ministry became a model, not only for other growing churches wanting to provide similar opportunities for their women, but also for the men.

I say this not because I believe we deserve credit for having done something remarkably extraordinary. Everything we did was either taken or adapted or inspired from somewhere else. Jesus's clear charge to us all is that we make disciples everywhere of everyone, and he told us how to do it. Where our churches sometimes struggle, however, is that we lose that focus. We get busy in many good activities, programs, and polity at the expense of doing the beautifully ordinary (although not always easy), daily undertaking of loving and building up of its people. All its people. Men and women.

Apparently, Aristotle was married twice but got too busy to count either of his wives' teeth or consult the Old Testament scrolls. The God of the universe has a vastly different, much more accurate, and decidedly more exalted view of women than our friend Aristotle. Having created us as fellow image-bearers, co-regents, and equal heirs with our male counterparts, God's plan is for each of us to know him intimately, to grow into his likeness, and to spread his glory in both male and female ways. Without that full expression, the whole church suffers.

It is essential then, that we teach, train, mentor, and cultivate opportunities for women to flourish for the glory of God and his church. Women's maturity as believers must matter to us because it matters so much to God.

I will share with you everything I can think of that we did to provide opportunities for women to grow, how we did it, and why. It's my prayer that you can take what's on these pages and use it to the great benefit of women and the entire body of Christ to the glory of God.

REVIEW AND DISCUSS

1. Does your view of women, (and yourself as a woman) more closely resemble God's view or Aristotle's? What consequences might the wrong view result in, for you personally, for your relationships, and for the church? Why is adopting God's view so vital?

2. Ephesians 4:15–16 makes it clear that every member of the body of Christ has an essential part to play in the growth and maturity of the church as a whole. Is this the reality in your

experience? What role might you play in building up other women?

3. Are you cognizant of your God-given gifts and abilities? How might you develop and use them for God's glory and the good of his church?

4. In speaking of God, Abigail Dodds wrote, "Man and woman are his image. But as women, we have the privilege of fully expressing our part. Without our full expression of it, we rob God of his full glory." Do you agree? How do you reflect God's image as a female?

CHAPTER 2

Starting "There": Beginning with the End in Mind

I SAT RECENTLY WITH a very capable woman who had just stepped into the role of women's ministry director at her church, and she had a valid and appropriate question for me. "How do I decide what to do? There's nothing much going on for women, so where do I start?"

There are actually two right answers to that question.

You start with where you want to go. And you start with where you are. Both are necessary beginnings. Both are important in discerning God's will and ways for your ministry. And both will need you to ask some important decision-determining questions.

Let's take the first one first. *Start with where you want to go.* It's always wise to begin with the end in mind.

A few months back, I spent the morning with one of my young grandsons. I listened intently as he explained all the intricacies of a new board game we were about to play together.

"There are cards and we put the cards here and some of them are good and some of them are bad. You don't want the bad ones, Nana."

Okay . . .

"And you have to move around the board and collect these badges. I'm going to try to get lots of badges, but just certain ones, not all of them."

Alright.

"And you have to have a game piece. Do you want to be red, yellow, green, or blue?"

Um, maybe blue . . .

"Great! I'll start."

Helpless doesn't even begin to describe my state of mind as I tried unsuccessfully to locate the instructions. But with his vast experience of having played the game (once) before and his inclusion of more than a few made-up rules, he somehow helped me get my game piece from the start to the middle until, mercifully, snack time interrupted our activity. That's one way to figure out what to do. I'd like to suggest another.

Start with the "object of the game." Begin by thinking through where it is you're trying to go, what you're trying to accomplish. The object of the game is the big, overarching purpose and it must set the trajectory for the ministry.

The question to ask here is: What's the end game in the life of a Christian? Where is God taking us? When all is said and done, where does he want us to be?

Throughout his Word, God instructs us in what is most important to him. His goal for us is an intertwined three-fold one.

God longs for us to know him as he is.

God wants us to become more like him.

God desires for us to spread his fame.

Let's take these one at a time.

GOD LONGS FOR US TO KNOW HIM AS HE IS.

Whatever other virtues or abilities we may possess or display, our understanding of God is primary. He explains it this way in his words to Jeremiah:

"The wise person should not boast in his wisdom; the strong person should not boast in his strength; the wealthy person should not boast in his wealth. But the one who boasts should boast in this, that he understands and knows me—that I am the Lord, showing faithful love, justice, and righteousness on the earth, for I delight in these things. This is the Lord's declaration." (Jer. 9:23–24)

Knowing God—his faithful love, his unparalleled justice, and his perfect righteousness—is what God wants for us. It's where he's trying to take us on our lifelong journey with him. Our knowledge of God shapes and informs us. It turns on the light in many a dark place.

Sadly, most of us are guilty of forming our ideas of God through other, varied means: song lyrics ("the little Lord Jesus no crying he makes," really??), stories we heard as a child, books, traditions, quips, and quotes about "the man upstairs," our own imaginations, and many more. But God has provided the way for us to have an accurate picture of him. He has revealed himself through his Word and through his Son. His

Spirit inspired human authors to record for all time a revelation of himself in his Word, describing his character, his motivations, and his works so that we would know him as he is. And he became flesh in the person of Jesus, so that we could see him, hear him, witness his interactions, and get a glimpse of just how far his love for us would go.

Each time I read through the Bible, I can't get over how repeatedly and often God makes crystal clear what he is like by revealing the motives of his interactions with us. He does what he does in the way that he does it so that we will know him! Using a variety of wordings and images, God tells us that he helps, he loves, he disciplines, he blesses, he teaches, and he changes people so that "then they will know that I am the LORD" (Ezek. 6:14 and many other verses). And he does so not out of his own vain self-interest, but for our very best. A right view of God will enable us to have a right view of ourselves, a right view of the world in which we live, and a right view of the circumstances we face. Ultimately, a right view of God will direct our paths as we lead others. J. I. Packer says it beautifully:

> Knowing about God is crucially important
> for the living of our lives. . . . We are cruel

to ourselves if we try to live in this world without knowing about the God whose world it is and who runs it. The world becomes a strange, mad, painful place, and life in it a disappointing and unpleasant business, for those who do not know about God. Disregard the study of God, and you sentence yourself to stumble and blunder through life, blindfold, as it were, with no sense of direction and no understanding of what surrounds you. This way you can waste your life and lose your soul.[1]

As we design plans, programs, and ministries for women, we must keep in mind that their purpose is to aid us in bringing women to a greater and truer understanding of God's character, motivations, and works. Everything we do should help us reach this goal in some way. We can think of it as a road trip, always aware of our final destination, so we don't get sidetracked and end up out of gas on some dead-end street somewhere!

GOD WANTS US TO BECOME MORE LIKE HIM.

Along with God's longing for us to know him as he is, he makes clear a second of his goals for us: that we would become more like him. This process, called *sanctification*, can be defined as "the cooperative work of God and Christians (Phil. 2:12–13) by which ongoing transformation into greater Christlikeness occurs. Such maturing transpires particularly through the Holy Spirit (2 Cor. 3:18; Gal. 5:16–23) and the Word of God (John 17:17)."[2]

The apostle John explains a mysterious truth about this sanctification process which should deepen our commitment to our first step of knowing God. The act of beholding God as he is transforms us.

> Dear friends, we are God's children now, and what we will be has not yet been revealed. We know that when he appears, we will be like him *because we will see him as he is*. (1 John 3:2, emphasis added)

One day, just seeing Jesus in all his glory, goodness, and majesty will change us into his likeness!

But Jesus hasn't returned to reappear face-to-face for us yet. So in the waiting time, we are urged to keep looking and keep seeking an ever clearer and truer view of him. We do that by feeding on his Word and availing ourselves of his indwelling change agent: the Holy Spirit. This, he tells us, is part of the process he uses to sanctify us. As we feast on his Word, God's Holy Spirit works in us to enable our motivations, thoughts, desires, words, and actions to be more like his.

The Spirit, who indwells us when we put our trust in Jesus as our Savior, works with God's written Word in pointing out our sin and leading us to turn from it. He reveals to us the weight of our wrongs and uses the Word to instruct us in what is true. He unveils to us the incomparable beauty of his grace, and enables us to experience God's forgiveness, comfort, gifting, and guidance. He softens our hearts to resemble God's heart and stirs in us a sincere love for him. The Holy Spirit produces in us qualities that are his: his love, his joy, his peace, his patience, his kindness, his goodness, his faithfulness, his gentleness, and his self-control (Gal. 5:22–23).

God's Spirit makes it possible for us to walk in his Word-explained ways! As we think and plan how to lead others, their spiritual maturity—that they are becoming more and more like the God they serve—must be our central aim. Keeping this objective front and center is invaluable in determining our priorities and programs. This is a clear "object of the game." All we offer should in some way create the atmosphere for and contribute to this end. This was Paul's stated purpose, his "so that," as he wrote to the church in Colossae. "We proclaim him, warning and teaching everyone with all wisdom, so that we may present everyone mature in Christ" (Col. 1:28).

Where does God want us to go? What's the end to keep in mind as we begin? Mature Christlikeness stemming from an ever-growing knowledge and love of God.

GOD DESIRES FOR US TO SPREAD HIS FAME.

God longs for us to know him and become more like him. Then thirdly, he desires for us to spread his fame. God tells us that we are created by him for his glory (Isa. 43:7), which can also be called his fame. As John Piper so lucidly explains, God's glory or fame is the "going public of his infinite worth."[3]

God wants all people everywhere to spread his fame so that all people everywhere know his infinite worth. He is great and good and wise and loving and just and perfect in every way! It is to our great detriment, and devastating to the world, to miss out on this realization.

As believers, how we conduct ourselves puts on display the God to whom we belong. The way we interact with others invokes in people's minds an image of our God. The way we deal with our own shortcomings, handle disappointments, and walk through hardships all reveal what we believe to be true about God. How we respond to life's circumstances shows what we consider real about our world and the trust we have in the character of God who is sovereign over it.

We can help women give thought to the God they are making public by raising questions such as:

- As others see how you live your life, what image does it conjure up in their minds about God?
- Do you display the character of God in your home and in your closest relationships?
- How can you encourage other women to labor for God's fame?

- What opportunities to make God famous are you missing at work? In your neighborhood?

This focus on God's fame, not our own, helps us put our work for God in its rightful place. God's fame shouts at us, "THIS IS NOT ABOUT YOU!" We are very small players in God's very big story, not the other way around. Our purpose is not to promote our own fame, or even to be gloriously remembered or loved. Our purpose is for God's fame to fill the whole earth. We do this through who we are, how we act, and what we say.

We need to help all women recognize and live into their created purpose of making God, in all his glory, famous. We do it by reminding them that this purpose can be realized, not only in our "right" moments, but also in our "wrong" ones. Women must know that God doesn't seek perfect people to use (he knows better), but rather he seeks to use those who are living for his glory instead of their own. We don't spread God's fame because we're perfect. We spread God's fame because *he is*.

Thus, we make God's righteousness famous by doing what is right in every circumstance. AND by pointing out that God does what's right even when we've just blown it. We make God's love famous by loving all others unconditionally. AND by openly confessing our own self-centeredness when we don't. We make God's mercy famous by forgiving others when we've been wronged. AND by experiencing God's forgiveness ourselves when we've made a mess of things. We make God's goodness famous when we repay evil with good. AND when we stop pretending we're perfect Christians but honestly admit our shortcomings, because only God is perfectly good.

Whether we think and behave like the sinners that we are or like the saints that God saved us and empowers us to be, we can spread God's fame. We can and must highlight God's character and his awesome works, whether we are mirroring them or falling very far short.

As we mentor and teach women, returning often to this foundational purpose is essential. Our egos so easily get in the way, and then we begin to work for our own renown instead of his. We compete and compare, resulting in pride, bitterness, jealousy, or insecurity. But putting God's fame above all else will give glory to whom it is due and abundant joy to the rest of us! When we keep God's fame the main thing, he has a mysterious way of highlighting our individuality, diverse gifts, and varied talents. He then underscores the beautiful reality that there is a place, space, purpose, and need for each of us in his church.

If we truly know him as he is, continue growing into his likeness, and live out the good news of his love and grace in all of our interactions, God's infinite worth will go public!

Whether you're meeting with a few women in your neighborhood or designing a program for all the women in your church, this is most certainly one necessary place to start: full recognition of where you're going. You are constantly moving toward a greater knowledge of God, growing in Christlikeness, and expanding the spread of his fame.

In the next chapter you'll find ideas and plans specifically designed to help reach our three aims. We'll discuss a God-centered Bible study, offer questions to ask as we go to God's Word daily, share ideas for a course on theology and practice, and suggest inserting a "God in focus" element in every teaching.

REVIEW AND DISCUSS

1. Keeping the destination in mind enables us to get to where we're going. Knowing God, becoming like him, and spreading his fame are goals God has laid out for us in his Word. Are you making progress in these areas? How can you help others grow towards these ends?

2. Are you forming a true picture of God through a deepening knowledge of his Word? How do you think an increased understanding of him affects the way you view your circumstances? Your relationships?

3. In this chapter, the question was raised, "As others see how you live your life, what image does it conjure up in their minds about God?" How would you answer this?

4. What opportunities are you or could you take to encourage others to spread God's fame? How would you respond to someone who claims to be too imperfect to spread God's fame?

CHAPTER 3

How to Get "There"

HAVING A CLEAR VISION of our end goal as we help move women toward spiritual maturity is essential. Then comes the plan—the "how to get there"—as we route our way to the destination God has laid out for us. If you're headed northwest to Seattle, Washington, from Louisville, Kentucky, you don't map out your travels toward the southeast through Atlanta, Georgia. (Unless of course you're flying Delta, then that may be, unfortunately, your only option!) Knowing where you're headed leads to countless possibilities regarding the path you take. It's also a huge help in eliminating some unhelpful options.

Our goals of 1) knowing God, 2) becoming like him, and 3) spreading his fame determine what we do and don't do. And keeping the end in mind will lead us to choose certain emphases over others. I'd like to share some examples with you of ways to help reach your destination. As you get to know the woman or women you are helping to grow, you'll likely come up with other ways—different routes, if you will—to get to the same place. But the clear "there" will help you navigate well, keep you moving in the right direction, and enable you to avoid countless detours.

DISCIPLESHIP—FOR 1 OR 100

Discipleship is the word commonly used to describe a journey of spiritual growth, where a teacher, or many varied teachers, impact a learner so that she grows and changes. It's a school of sorts, but it isn't just memory work or head knowledge. It's designed to help us:

1. think God's thoughts after him.
2. have our hearts molded and shaped by God's Word and his Spirit.
3. be used of God to spread his fame.

TRUTH BE TOLD—EXAMPLES OF TEACHING DOCTRINE

Providing an overview of the foundational truths and practices in our lives as believers lays the groundwork in reaching all three of our aims as we disciple others.

These held truths, or doctrines, help us to get a right picture of God, his work, and his plans, and give us a correct view of ourselves. Important practices established in our daily lives enable the truth to shape us and help transform us into instruments for God's use. And being used of God grows our dependence on him and increases our faith.

All of this takes time. Truth doesn't take root, nor are our hearts and minds transformed, overnight. Be patient with yourself and the growth process in others. There's no sacred order to laying the foundation for helping others grow . . . except for the Cornerstone, Jesus! You can be somewhat flexible with all the other building blocks. Having said that, intentionality with a plan is always good. You have to start somewhere, so here's one beginning.

PRACTICALLY SPEAKING: EXAMPLE 1

Using a guide to help you, cover all the basic doctrines of the Christian faith, like the attributes of God, the person and work of Christ, who the Holy Spirit is and why he came, the Word of God, the Trinity, and more. Once followers of Christ have said "yes" to him and have a basic grasp of the gospel, supplying them with a fuller and deeper understanding of who God is, what he has done, and what he has for them is a tremendous gift! I have used the book *Life's Biggest Questions* by Erik Thoennes to serve as a text to provide solid teaching and truth about most doctrinal topics to cover.[1] Another book by my favorite author and husband, *50 Core Truths of the Christian Faith*, is a great resource to help you lead others in imparting these ideas, including pitfalls you'll want to avoid.[2] Still a third book, longer and treating the topics in more depth, is *Bible Doctrines* by Wayne Grudem.[3] An eight-week study titled, *Everyday Theology: What You Believe Matters*, by Mary Wiley covers important doctrines in a very approachable way.[4] And finally, *You Are a Theologian*, by Jen Wilkin and J. T. English offers a clear and very applicable treatment of the doctrines.[5]

Whatever book you choose, if you are working with an individual or small group, you can read a chapter together, look up the Bible passages referenced, go through the questions included in each chapter, help each other apply what you're learning, and grow together! A constant reminder in all of this: You are deepening your head and heart knowledge of a personal triune God—your Lord, Savior, and Guide—not just learning abstract truths about him. You are growing a relationship with a living God, Father, Shepherd, Teacher, Friend, and Provider—just to name a few of his roles and identities. As you disciple others in doctrinal truths, keep your intimate devotion to God central.

THINGS TO CONSIDER FOR A LARGE GROUP

If you're discipling a large group of women through doctrines and practices, you'll have a "discipleship school" of sorts. Due to greater numbers, you'll need to organize and delegate so that each woman still receives personal attention, input, and accountability. In Appendix 1, you'll find a sample syllabus for a "Discipleship School," a twenty-four-week curriculum, designed for a large group of women. You could also use it as a road map to journey with one or a small group of women.

Whether you have a large group or a small one, your goals are the same. With the larger group, however, you will need to formalize the process on the front end so that each woman is known and cared for, which is so important in our growth process. You will need to focus on a few: that is, select and disciple several women who will in turn be the leaders or overseers of their own small groups. In this way, each woman participating is seen and heard. Pour into your "few" and model for them how they are to invest in the women in their groups. The interest and the enthusiasm of those you are focusing on, their love for God and his Word, and their application of what they are learning will be contagious to all the women in their groups.

With a larger group and greater resources, I recommend planning out your entire course in advance and recruiting teachers for each lesson. Offer live instruction to the whole group on the doctrine taught by capable teachers. Then follow up the teaching time with discussion on the topic in your smaller groups at tables or circles around the room. The group time is vital in helping the women grow in their understanding and application of what was taught, as they interact with the material through questions, answers, and discussion.

Prior to the start of your "school," the small group leaders should receive training in how to facilitate a discussion, handle difficult questions, keep the conversation on track, and graciously hold the women accountable. You'll find some suggested training material in Appendix 2 (which applies to leading a Bible study or discipleship school discussion) and more information about helping women lead in chapter 7. You may find, as I did, that your group leaders ask to lead again the subsequent time Discipleship School is offered and women who have completed Discipleship School volunteer to repeat it by becoming group leaders. They benefit greatly as they are taught God's truth, glean insights from the women in their groups, and grow to be better facilitators.

One possible pitfall of your large group "Discipleship School" with its need for greater organization and structure is the danger of losing sight of your goal. Your goal is growth in the people, not the program. Take care to keep the "there" in mind! You want each individual to grow in her knowledge of God, to become more like him, and to spread his fame. The goal is NOT for women to finish the course or "graduate" from your discipleship school. It is not mere head knowledge of doctrinal truth or the completion of practical assignments. It is not information, but transformation. Truth and practice are necessary, and knowledge is valuable. But they are the *means*, while hearts and minds transformed, and God's glory displayed are the goals.

WHETHER A LARGE OR SMALL GROUP

Include with the doctrines taught practical means for your disciple to know God, be changed by him, and spread his fame. Teach her how to study the Bible, how to share her story, and how to talk about the gospel. Help her to establish regular times in God's Word and in prayer. And help her to know God's love for her and his gifts to her.

An additional component which should be included, whether you are working with one woman or one hundred, is the "pass-it-on" piece. Always look to the future as you lead the women in front of you. You can think about this in two ways. 1) Focus on the immediate future by encouraging every woman to share what's she's learning with someone else. Help her choose a "disciple." She can simply share a sentence or two of what she has learned with her roommate, spouse, or child. Or she can open the Bible with a friend and explain what she has discovered about the goodness of God or the character of Jesus. 2) Keep in mind also the months and years ahead. Right from the start, teach and train your disciples with the intention that one day they will have their own disciples and be passing on what they are learning to others. Give them tools to help them lead; share insights about handling questions or dealing with issues as they arise; relay what you are learning from God's Word and how you learned it. Teach your disciples to be disciplers.

Spreading God's fame fuels our growth and is a beautiful part of God's plan to expand his renown.

PRACTICALLY SPEAKING: EXAMPLE 2

Rather than using a book as a resource to guide you through your doctrinal study, you can take women directly to God's Word as the basis for your teaching. You'll still be looking at the character of God, Jesus Christ, the Holy Spirit, and more. For every topic, passages of Scripture can guide you as you ask exploratory questions of the text. The pros of this is that you will go directly to God's Word to discover what he has to say about who he is and what he has done. At the same time, you are also familiarizing your disciple with the Bible and modeling how to go straight to the source to learn truth. This method is most effective when used one-on-one or with a small group. Unlike Example 1, more responsibility rests with you as the "teacher." A disciple will tend to look to you for answers where she finds the Scriptures unclear or difficult for her to understand. If you are equipped to lead in this way, great! If you are unsure, you can either choose to use the book-as-guide method in Example 1 or use this method while using one of the books suggested in the first example as a resource for you as you lead.

In Appendix 1, I've included an example of a "Scriptural Guide for Discipleship" with passages of Scripture and questions designed to lead your disciple into a knowledge of God and his ways. You can use this simple eight session guide as is, or as a starting point to develop your own, covering additional topics. To encourage understanding and retention, I recommend you ask women to record each lesson's discoveries, applications, and prayers in a notebook, journal, or electronic device, and then talk about them with you. As you meet, ask each other how God is revealing himself and his character.

Encourage each other to apply the truths of who God is to the way you view yourselves, others, and your circumstances.

HEARTS SHAPED—GUIDING OTHERS TO SEE AND KNOW GOD

God promises that the good work he started in us when we first became believers—molding and shaping us into his likeness—he will complete (Phil. 1:6). We can be really excited about this because God does great work! And strange as it may seem, he has chosen to give us a part in this sanctifying work. He urges us to *pursue* Christlikeness. The apostle Paul tells his disciple, Timothy, "train yourself in godliness" (1 Tim. 4:7).

In leading women toward spiritual maturity, it's important that we provide them with instructions on how to develop good "training" habits. Training takes consistent practice to produce effective results. A growing, intimate, life-altering relationship with God requires time spent with him and input from him. Resources are in great supply which explain "spiritual disciplines" and "spiritual formation practices," all which have as their goal a deeper knowledge of God and greater Christlikeness in our lives. I've listed a few of these resources in the Notes.[6]

As we disciple others, we can begin by encouraging them to establish regular "meetings" with God, listening to God as he speaks through his Word, and talking to him as they pray. Make sure, as you encourage, you instruct. Explain what a devotional or "quiet time" with God might look like. Give them ideas for what to do and how to proceed. If step one is to open their Bible, then point them to step two! God says that his Word is living and active (Heb. 4:12), but it can quickly feel flat and stagnant without adequate direction. Mere box-checking to fulfill our "quiet time requirement" is neither glorifying to God nor beneficial to his children.

One method I've found helpful in breathing life into a daily devotional time, is asking questions of myself and God as I read his Word. When I'm reading in the Gospels, I ask myself what I think the original audience would have found surprising or confusing about what Jesus did or said. Then I ask myself what *I* find surprising or confusing. I tell Jesus that I'm confused, and my confusion becomes a matter of prayer. I ask him to bring clarity and help me understand. I pay special attention to what the passage reveals about the heart of Jesus and how different my heart is. Then I often tear up and always ask him to change and shape my heart to be more like his.

As I read any passage in the Bible, I ask God to show me his character and his ways. And then I ask myself, in light of this truth about God, how should it affect the way I view my current circumstances or situation? Sometimes I tell him what makes me uncomfortable about what I just read and then I ask him about that. And I ask him to change my mind and mold my will when I clearly have different views and desires than he does. I thank him that I can talk to him and that he invites my questions. Then I ask him if we can do this again tomorrow.

In Appendix 3, you will find a sampling of some questions (entitled "Devotional Questions") designed to help women get to know Jesus better, grow in their knowledge of God, and spawn conversations with him. You can add to them or write your own, but whether you're leading one woman or many, helping them learn to interact daily with honest curiosity with our living God through his active Word is heart-shaping!

WISDOM GAINED—SUGGESTIONS FOR BIBLE STUDY

Another essential component in our discipleship of women is teaching them how to study and glean truth from

God's Word. Many helpful books provide instruction and insights into methods for effective Bible study and application. I've included a few highly recommended resources in the Notes.[7] In our Discipleship School curriculum, we devote several weeks to teaching women the foundational "how-tos" of Bible study. It's an essential component in helping women grow to maturity. A few weeks, however, are not a substitute for an on-going, in-depth study of God's Word together with women to teach and enable them to "catch" how to approach, study, and apply the Scriptures in their lives.

I'd like to offer some suggestions which, whether you've taken on the task of leading a large group study or are hosting a small study in your home, may be helpful.

1. Look for the Who of the Bible, as you see the What. It is valuable to learn about the history of our faith, the successes and failures of our predecessors, and the promises for our future. We are encouraged to discover stories of great courage and hold onto verses which comfort or embolden us. We love to seek out God's plans for us and hunt for help in our decision-making. All these aims must never, however, be ends unto themselves. Our goal in our exploration of God's Word is a knowledge of God himself. The Author is the subject and the hero of this book! Train yourself and others to look for God on every page of the Bible. He has chosen to reveal himself through his inspired Word, and we are wise to listen closely. Thus, a question at every Bible study opportunity is, "What do we see about God in this section?"

2. Study books of the Bible, not books about books of the Bible. The "original source," or more colloquially, "directly from the horse's mouth," is where we are always pointed when we're trying to understand an author's intent and meaning. This advice is even more vital when we're dealing with God and his written Word. God's Spirit inspired the Bible's human authors to inscribe the words and include the poems, stories, instructions, visions, commands, and details as he so-willed. His Spirit then illumines us as we read the Word to understand and apply it to our lives. What others write about the Word is interesting and can be quite helpful, but God's Word itself is alive and transformational. It not only teaches us, but it does the work in us of heart renovation. Make sure your Bible study is a study of the Bible.

3. Use teachers that are locally grown, not imported. Whenever possible—and from my experience it is always more possible than we think—select women from your own context

47

to teach the Word rather than regularly using a video teaching "expert." I say this for several reasons. First, while highly respecting and having learned a good deal from some of our well-known Bible teachers on video, this is a matter of priority, not preference. I may prefer to hear a polished teaching from a world-class communicator rather than a rough-edged lesson from a less-experienced woman in my congregation. But that less-experienced woman will forever remain so unless she gains experience! In a later chapter we'll look at raising up leaders and teachers, but it is important here to note this fact. Although with "locally grown" teachers there may be growing pains, growth rarely happens without the pains, and growth is vital. It takes time and it is work, yes, but it is God's plan to give gifts to his children. Then he desires that those children develop and use his gifts to "promote the growth of the body for building itself up in love" (Eph. 4:16).

Second, although you, the reader, may be an outstanding Bible teacher, never neglect your responsibility to step away from your lectern and allow others to teach the Bible. A danger in using just one skilled teacher is two-fold. Not only does it eliminate the possibility of others gaining experience, but it can also communicate that there is one best way to teach through one certain style and personality. God used David's poetry, Moses's stories, Paul's treatises, and many others to teach us and transmit his truth. Model good teaching practices expressed through your personality. Then seek out those faithful women whom God has gifted and prepare them to spread his fame as they "teach others also" (2 Tim. 2:2).

4. Keep zooming in and zooming out. There are no weeds in the Bible, but I've been to more than a few Bible studies in which we seemed to have been lost in them! Details are good, and we gain valuable insights as we notice and ponder the Bible's particulars. Thus, we must take the time and care to zoom in and examine the fine points—each and every God-breathed word. But unless we also regularly zoom out as we study Scripture, we can easily get lost in the minutiae. The Bible is one big story, a metanarrative, and each of its books, chapters, and verses in some way contribute to that story. As we teach the Bible and focus in on the facts, features, and specific elements within individual books, we need to take special care to note the overarching point the author's trying to make. What has the Holy Spirit inspired the human author to communicate? What is Moses persuading us to understand and believe? What does Paul not want us to miss? Whatever that is, as we teach, we need to zoom out to help women see it. We zoom in to see the details—the evidences that support and reveal to us the author's central argument. Then we zoom out again as we teach, to reveal God's primary message to us. Each word, verse, and chapter contains beautiful and significant truth for us to uncover. It's only as we see the details in their rightful place within the big picture, however, that they communicate God's true intent. Thoughtful, thorough, curious, and Spirit-dependent Bible study which is both detailed and telescopic will enable us to think God's thoughts after him and have our hearts shaped by him.

You will find question sheets for various genres of Scripture to aid you in zooming in to notice the smallest details and zooming out to see how those details support the overarching teaching of the passage by visiting bhpublishinggroup.com/AShortGuidetoWomensMinistry. These have proved very helpful in arriving at an accurate interpretation and application of the passage studied.

5. Expect growth to take time. Spiritual growth is beautiful and enduring, but it's not easy or instantaneous.

It takes time to get God's Word into our hearts and minds. It takes time to change our ideas and grow our faith.

It takes time to understand new concepts and incorporate them into our thinking and behavior. God is well-aware of our growth rate and is patient with each one of us. We, too, must be patient with ourselves and those we teach and lead.

As you design your Bible study, build in times for the women to read and ponder God's Word (think: interesting homework!) as well as times to discuss what they've studied. Encourage them to ask their questions and share their thoughts. Processing, personally and with others, aids significantly in our understanding and "absorption" of what we're learning. Help women with creative ways to spend time in God's Word on their own—podcasts in the car, an open Bible in every room, phone reminders to meditate on Scripture, verses on their mirrors and refrigerators, accountability partners, and more. At the same time, recognize that we all go through seasons of strained schedules and stress-filled situations. Grace comes first. Attending a Bible study without advance preparation is way better than not attending at all, so love each of your participants well. Pray that every woman will grow in thinking God's thoughts after him, have her heart molded by God's Word, and be used of God to spread his fame. And then adjust your expectations to include time.

REVIEW AND DISCUSS

1. Have you considered or are you currently involved in a doctrinal study personally or with others? How might learning and teaching God's character, works, and ways be transformational in your life and in the lives of others?

2. Whether you're helping to lead one woman or a large group of women, how can you make sure each person is known and cared for? What steps can you take to not lose sight of God's goals for her? How can you grow in patience with yourself and others, knowing that growth takes time?

3. As we help others grow in their Christian lives, the "pass-it-on" piece is vital. How are you encouraging others to share what they're learning and preparing them to become disciple-makers themselves?

4. Going directly to God in his Word through devotional times and Bible study is foundational to our growth and intimacy with God. How are you honing your skills in observing, interpreting, and applying the Scriptures? Are you looking for God as you read?

CHAPTER 4

Starting "Here": Beginning Where You Are

WITH DAUGHTERS IN SEATTLE and France, I'm always looking for great deals on airline tickets to both destinations. I get excited when an email's subject line boasts an impressive offer coming into my inbox. The problem is, those bargain flights always seem to take off from New York or Chicago, Dallas, or London . . . and I live in Louisville, Kentucky. The "great deal" quickly reveals itself to be not-so-great after all because I can't leave from there when I live here! I need to begin my journey where I am.

When we brainstorm to reach our God-inspired ends, we often strategize programs and methodologies focused on our great goals. We design grand plans for lofty outcomes. We know where God wants to take us, so we envision elaborate means and structures to get us there. It's good, even admirable, to have a big vision, but we must begin where we are to realize God's plans for us.

Many start-of-the-year planning sessions I've been a part of have posed this question: If there were no limits to your resources (time, money, space, gifted individuals), what would you do? These exercises were designed to help me dream big and trust God to supply all that I need. And many unrestrained, creative ideas would result from my brainstorming. The weakness in this approach, however, is that we *do* have limited resources—God-ordained ones—and not taking them into account can cause us to miss the beauty of God's inauspicious beginnings and the real-life paths he wants us to take. His goals for us are grand indeed, but his methods of getting there are almost always humble and unpretentious. He created us and the world in which we live with limits. We can't be everywhere; we can't do everything; and getting to know God and growing to be like him doesn't happen overnight.

We were born at a particular time in a particular place in a limited human body. This was God's plan from the beginning and it's *good*. He has chosen to use the limited, the seemingly insufficient, the unexpected, and the unremarkable to show his glory. He wants us to walk with him moment-by-moment, pay attention to where we are, begin with what he has provided, and trust him with the outwardly little we have to work with. Taking inventory of our limited resources, giving thanks for them, being intentional with them, and asking God to use them as he wills is our starting place.

Jesus modeled this for us in countless ways. He could have asked his Father to rain manna or quail on his five thousand–plus hungry listeners, but he chose to focus the disciples' attention on the provision they did have: five loaves and two fish. After Jesus thanked his Father for multiplying his small supply, the entire crowd ate its fill, and each disciple had a doggy bag to take home with him (Mark 6:35–43).

Jesus could have spread the good news of his kingdom in a more impressive, efficient way. He could have stepped into time *after* the creation of the internet. He could have begun his ministry with prominent, powerful leaders—kings and rabbis—who could have used their wealth and authority to impact many more to listen and follow. Or he could have at least prepared and chosen followers who were educated, trained, and influential instead of the ragtag bunch he actually chose (Acts 4:13). Had he preferred, Jesus could have healed every lame and blind person in every crowd instantaneously with a wave of his hand or a word from his mouth. He elected, instead, to use a one-at-a-time, personal method, leaving some still physically unrestored.

God could have sent Jesus as an adult, ready for ministry, instead of playing the long game with a thirty-year growth gap between the heavenly host's nighttime declaration to the shepherds and John the Baptist's "Lamb of God" pronouncement.

God's ways are not our ways. He has a history of accomplishing supremely significant outcomes from meager means and seemingly inconsequential people. He starts with what he has and where we are—untrained, often surprisingly "average," and sometimes very ill-equipped individuals—and uses us in doing his magnificent will.

God drives this fact home in an impressive way in one of Israel's famous battles (Judg. 6–7). God's chosen leader at the time, insecure, skeptical Gideon, was instructed to drive the powerful Midianites from the land that God had promised to the Israelites. When Gideon was finally ready to obey God, he still had one slight problem. He had *too many* men in his army—thirty-two thousand, to be exact. After Gideon whittled the number down to just ten thousand fighting men, God still did not approve. Only after they shrunk their numbers to three hundred—armed only with trumpets and glass jars holding torches—did God give the go-ahead to Gideon to confront Midian's army. God preferred to limit the numbers and provide unconventional resources. And he shares with us the reason behind his unusual strategy. He will save his people in this way, "or else Israel might elevate themselves over me and say, 'I saved myself'" (Judg. 7:2). Working within limits demonstrates the greatness and limitlessness of our God and will likely save us from prideful boasting.

> God has chosen what is foolish in the world to shame the wise, and God has chosen what is weak in the world to shame the strong. God has chosen what is insignificant and despised in the world—what is viewed as nothing—to bring to nothing what is viewed as something, so that no one may boast in his presence. (1 Cor. 1:27–29)

Whether you are a part of a large, vibrant church or a small, fledgling one, you will still crash up against limits. You'll have too many women for the teachers and mentors you have, too many kids for the childcare workers available, and too many needs for the time and money to meet them. Or, you'll have a vision for a school of discipleship, but no one else who shares your vision. You'll long to have a growing Bible study of enthusiastic women, but only one woman interested. You'll have a fabulous idea for a retreat, but no time to organize it or women to attend it. You'll have trained, eager women wanting to engage in the life of your church, but no leadership opportunities to offer to them. The list of limits is limitless!

The two most encouraging words in the Bible, however, are "But God." God uses what he has provided for us and, as we walk with him, does what he wants with it, to the praise of his glory.

Our "there"—the goal God has laid out for us—is leading others to know him, become like him, and spread his fame. Our goal has never been a successful program or a well-attended event. You may not have 100 women ready and willing to pursue him, but look around and start with the two that you have. You likely don't have ten trained mentors to launch ten mentoring groups next month but pray and ask the three or four in whom you see potential to join you and start a group of your own. Build into them and pray with and for them.

We will struggle in helping women know God, become like him, and spread his fame if we start with a program, even if we've seen that program proven successful elsewhere. Begin, instead, right where you are. Start with the people God has placed in front of you, with the gifts, desires, and natural abilities he has given them. Plan your program based on your people, not the other way around. There is more than one route to reach your goals, but all your routes must begin where you are. So first locate your "you are here." Who has God placed in your sphere of influence? Who has expressed a desire to grow? What resources are at your disposal as you plan? What burden has God laid on your heart?

When our "mother church" birthed a second congregation in the same city, I went from co-leading the women's ministry at a large established church to becoming the sole director at the new site. My initial desire was to duplicate a few of our proven women's initiatives with our start-up congregation. The problem was, I didn't have the same leaders with the same gifts, nor those with a similar vision. What I did have, were two women who independently shared with me their immense desire to launch and invest in a women's Bible study at our church. That's what we had, so that's where we started.

It was small and it was imperfect. But God honored our faith and obedience, and in a few years, that study grew in size and in depth, becoming a core ministry within our church. All glory to God.

Our limits are the framework within which God displays his limitless power, grace, and majesty. Embrace your "here" and then look for his glory to shine.

In the next chapter you'll find some suggested methods to help discern "where you are" and some beginning steps to take from there.

REVIEW AND DISCUSS

1. God created us with limited bodies and limited capacities, and placed us in limited spaces, with limited resources. Have you considered your limits as gifts from God? How might embracing your limits positively affect your life and ministry?

2. We looked at examples of how God displayed his greatness through people's limitations and how he chose the weak in the world to show his strength. Do you see your frailties

as opportunities for God's glory to shine? Have you ever witnessed God's power revealed through human weakness? What was that like?

3. Are you aware of the particular resources that you have been given—your time, abilities, means, and relationships? Are you thankful for them? Are you being intentional with them, asking God to use them as he wills?

4. Who has God placed in your sphere of influence? Who has indicated a hunger to know God and his Word? Take some time to locate the "you are here" starting point of these you might help to grow spiritually. What plan can you come up with which begins right where you are?

CHAPTER 5

How to Start "Here"

WHENEVER WE TRY TO figure out the best route to our destination, whether we're looking at a mall map or a hiking trail diagram, the marker we always seek out first is the one that says, "You Are Here." Though we know exactly where we want to go and can even point to it on the map, deciding how to get there becomes next to impossible unless we know where we're starting *from*. Where we are determines which path we need to take to get there. Similarly, we may have clear in our minds God's goals for the women we are discipling, but until we figure out where they are now, we will have a difficult time deciding which direction to go and how best to use the resources God has provided.

KNOW YOUR CHURCH

If you are working with women within a church context, it's important to first ascertain the "You Are Here" starting point of your church. If you simply assume your church has the same vision, values, and excitement about your ministry ideas as you do, you may end up disappointed or frustrated. Request a meeting with your pastor or a ministry leader to ask questions about your church's mission and vision, about what your church values, and about how to work within the church's structure. You will want to find out what ministries already exist, what purposes they are serving, and what needs are still present. How would someone go about beginning a new ministry at your church? Do most programs and ideas come from the "top," or do the leaders encourage grass roots initiatives? How does the church respond to women starting and leading ministries? Where do initiatives for women fit into the overall vision of the church?

In your meeting, ask your questions respectfully and be a good listener. You may or may not be excited about the answers to all your questions, but you will know where you are, and that's where you need to start. You may need to pray for more openness and opportunities for women. Or you may need to pray for more time in your week and more women to help you respond to all the occasions for ministry that are available for you to step into!

You will want to ask questions too, to ascertain the demographic of your church's neighborhood, or you may be in for a surprise. When a church in which I served relocated, the staff began brainstorming about outreaches to the children and parents in our new neighborhood. Only after a thorough assessment was done did we learn that the vast majority of those living nearby were empty nesters and a large percentage of those were widows and widowers. Our plans in spreading God's fame to our new neighbors changed from organizing moms' groups and play dates to offering lawn care, snow removal, and odd jobs for the elderly.

Our starting point for outreach at an urban church where I served was quite different. Getting to know our neighbors revealed many single moms in the immediate vicinity of the church. Thus, every other month we hosted a free oil change in our parking lot, complete with donuts and gracious conversations with moms and their kids as their cars were being serviced.

For both churches, spreading God's fame was the clear goal, but different starting points resulted in different approaches. It's best not to make plans or proposals until you know the reality you're stepping into.

KNOW YOUR CHURCH'S NEEDS

As you meet with leaders, listen carefully for needs that are expressed. Wherever you encounter a discrepancy between God's desires and the current reality of your church, you've uncovered a need. And the greater the discrepancy, the greater the need. For example, God wants widows and orphans to be cared for (James 1:27). Where they are not, there is a need. God wants us to pray about everything with thanksgiving (Phil. 4:6). Where instead there is complaining and prayerlessness, there is a need. God ordained marriages to be showcases of sacrificial love and respect (Eph. 5:33). Where there is brokenness, selfishness and strife, there is a need. God wants men and women to abide in his Word (John 8:31). Where they do not, there is a need. These needs and many more are the "You Are Here," markers, and may be right where God wants you to step in to serve, teach, or lead women in the church.

Communicate to your leadership your desire to help meet needs, not create more. Most likely, more meetings will be required, along with a good dose of patience, before a ministry will be approved and can be implemented, as church wheels often turn slowly. God is not on our time line, but he's never late. Use the waiting time to get to know individual women, identify their needs, and begin doing for a few what you hope to do for many. Then use your discoveries to plan next steps whenever God opens the door.

KNOW THE WOMEN

There's really only one best way to discover the "You Are Here" starting point of the women you want to disciple, regardless of whether you are a part of a large church or plan to meet with a few neighbors. You must get to know them. You must take the time necessary to meet with women one-on-one. Ask them lots of questions and listen to their stories. Find out where they've lived, what has shaped them, and what's most important to them. You may be surprised to discover where they are spiritually, what gifts and abilities they have, and what their struggles and needs are. Inquire about their daily lives, and the responsibilities they are carrying. Personal encounters will help you recognize that women will be at very different stages of life and different places in their relationships with God. Your questions may reveal a "pre-Christian" empty nester who needs to be introduced to the true, gentle, and winsome Jesus, or a young mom of preschoolers who is a new believer and needs more truth, a model of godliness, and lots of grace. You will likely discover a hurting believer who, after years of church-inflicted wounds, needs time, understanding, grace, and a listening ear. Or you may find mature, healthy believers of all ages and stages who are ready for training and ministry opportunities.

Meeting with women individually may seem time-consuming and inefficient, because it is! But nothing is more valuable or more effective. You will be connecting with fellow image bearers, getting to know them, and learning how you may be able to walk alongside them. The knowledge you gain and the relationships you build is the foundational starting point of all that follows.

KNOW THE WOMEN'S NEEDS

As you get to know the women you will begin to discover where they are in the lifelong process of reaching God's goals for them. Listen carefully for the needs that they express. You may meet a woman with a particular need one day and another woman who can meet that need the next day! You may talk to women who have gaps in their knowledge of God, their understanding of the Word, or their application of the gospel. Some may struggle with depression or battle with a recurring sin. Others may be in the middle of difficult relational conflicts. Or still others may be bursting with the desire to serve God but need direction in how to do so. The woman in front of you and the needs that you perceive reveal your starting point in sketching out the next steps in helping her grow. And don't be surprised if you make a new close friend or two in the process!

A young mom whom I was just getting to know approached me, asking if I would mentor her. I was glad to do so, but I had no idea what to do or where to start! We met a few times to talk, and as we did, her desires and needs became apparent. She knew that, in just one year's time, her husband would graduate from seminary, and she would likely become a pastor's wife. She saw her need to grow in her knowledge of God's Word, learn better how to study it, and have accountability for applying it to her life. And I also saw her need for dependance on God and confidence in his provision for the role he was calling her to step into. We decided to meet weekly to work through a book of the Bible, passage by passage, highlighting the character of God, skills for approaching the study of Scripture, personal application, and prayer. Knowing her needs, context, and concerns enabled us to design a time that was beneficial and encouraging. There are many different things we could have done, but identifying her need helped us pinpoint where to start and first steps to take.

As the women's ministry director, I knew that many young women in our church wished to be mentored. I also knew of two godly women who desired to launch a program for mentoring. It was necessary for me to discover if the one-to-one mentor to "mentee" program they were proposing would meet the needs of the younger women and be the best use of our church's resources. I was wondering too, if it would fit with the makeup and DNA of our church as well as be in keeping with the gifts of the two women making the proposal.

Though I was confident that mentoring relationships would be very beneficial in growing women into Christlikeness, I had to locate the "You Are Here" markers to know what types of structure, methods, and materials we should use. I asked the two women to pause moving forward with their proposed formal program so we could pray, think, and plan.

Knowing that we had an abundance of young women and a shortage of mature women at our church, I had doubts about the feasibility of a one-to-one mentoring model. I was already in the process of using a different format myself. I had previously formed a group with seven women each of whom had leadership responsibilities. I wanted to spend more time with them, discern their needs, and understand what was most helpful to them. I intentionally invited women who had different roles and were in various life stages, not only because they were incredible women, but also because they were representative of the women in our church as a whole. The group was composed of an empty nester (who was one of the two potential mentor ministry leaders), two single women, a young married woman without children, and three moms with kids of varying ages. As I got to know them better, certain common needs became evident. The most obvious need in these leaders was to have Christ-centered relationships where they could glean godly advice. They needed to be known and to deepen gospel-centered friendships. Second only to that was their need to be poured into, loved for who they were (rather than only what they "produced" as leaders), and regularly reminded of God's goodness in their lives. Our monthly meetings became a time I would pamper the women with snacks and desserts, pass on what God was teaching me, remind them of God's vision, give them space to share their joys and burdens, and take time to pray for one another. As our meetings continued, we would adjust the discussion topics to fit existential needs that became apparent. As long as the content was gospel-centered and relevant to their lives and ministry, the specific topics I introduced for our group were secondary. I learned from the women that mentoring in a group was very encouraging and effective in meeting their needs. It was also a practical necessity with our shortage of mature women! I became convinced that instead of an overly structured program, a more organic approach was very well-received and one we should pursue.

As I shared my insights with the two women who desired to lead the ministry, they paired up and started their own mentor group with women they wanted to pour into. Soon they were leading two groups. Currently, several groups led by women they have trained now meet using a variety of content: gospel-centered book discussions, discipleship fundamentals, Bible study helps, and more. In every group, the participants find a place to be known, loved, and to hear God's truth applied to their circumstances by older women who want to invest in them. At the same time, the leaders are expanding their influence and seeing their gifts used by God while also finding themselves at the receiving end of fulfilling relationships.

God sees us and communicates with us personally. We are wise to do the same with the women we meet. In Appendix 4, you'll find some suggested questions and ideas (entitled "Know the Women and Know Your Church"). In Appendix 5, there are tips and resources for mentor groups.

Investing the time necessary to get to know the women you are working with can't be overstated. And if we are ministering within a large church context, we must figure out how to meet and assess the needs of greater numbers of women. The urge to speed things up and simply gather factual information about women will always be a temptation! Online surveys are frequently a church's method of choice to obtain "relevant" data about people, their interests, and their gifts. And if your goal is acquiring data, a survey is effective. You can get to know facts about a woman through a questionnaire, but you don't get to know the woman. Her abilities, her personality, her hurts, her story will not come out of the boxes she checks. What brings tears to her eyes or causes them to light up with delight will be hidden to the reader of the survey—*if* her form actually gets read. Oh, how many times yours truly has waited in vain for any type of action or response to forms I submitted! Instead of meeting a woman on paper, meet her in person. Find out about her life, her walk with God, and her hopes for the future.

Where a broadly distributed survey can be of some help is in familiarizing you with the demographics of the women you are serving. This is valuable information for designing specific ministries and meeting times. A survey may allow you to finally "see" the women who are not there at any of the currently offered programs. Working and/or single moms, for example, will not be showing up at daytime Bible studies. Even evening studies and events, following a full workday, may be extremely challenging for them to attend. Without childcare available, single moms may have to miss every gathering. Don't assume that women are not interested in growing spiritually because they don't show up to your particular event. Put yourself in their places. Pay attention to their circumstances. Then schedule and plan around the needs of the women you hope to build into. Meeting online after kids' bedtimes or in the early morning hours using Zoom or Google Meet may be wise alternatives for those who work all day and have sleeping little ones.

Before you plan, and as you pray, take your time and put in the effort to pinpoint your "You Are Here" marker. Get to know your church. Get to know the women. Then start where you are.

REVIEW AND DISCUSS

1. Do you know the "you are here" reality of your church? What is its vision, its mission, and its values? What are its greatest needs and the needs of the surrounding neighborhood? In light of the needs you see, how might God be leading you to step in to meet them?

2. Asking questions and listening to answers is essential in getting to know women. How are you doing in the art of question-asking? What are some questions you can ask to help you better know and understand the people around you?

3. What do you see are the pros and cons of church surveys? When is a survey helpful and when may it actually prove to be hurtful?

4. We often begin ministry planning with a program idea rather than an individual's needs. What are some practical ways to turn this around, giving priority, as God does, to people over programs?

CHAPTER 6

Leadership Lessons: Hearts vs. Stars

FEW THINGS ARE AS mysterious as the human heart. Even though it remains completely hidden from view, we have identified the heart as the seat of our deepest thoughts, motivations, emotions, and affections. So much goes on in there that we can't see or understand! We hear words spoken and witness behaviors enacted, but the true self with its desires and intentions, good, bad, and neutral, are for the Lord's eyes only. And it is completely beyond our ability to predict which hearts, now hard, will become soft and pliable in God's hands or vice versa. How, then, do we rightly carry out the task of selecting those whom he desires to lead others in the service of his kingdom?

God made clear in his conversation with the prophet Samuel the criteria to avoid when choosing Israel's king.

The LORD said to Samuel, "Do not look at his appearance or his stature because I have rejected him. Humans do not see what the LORD sees, for humans see what is visible, but the LORD sees the heart." (1 Sam. 16:7)

God was warning Samuel that looks can be deceiving. Our five senses were designed by God to perceive the physical world. But when it comes to making decisions of a spiritual nature, those same senses may lead us astray. Only God can see the heart, thus following his criteria and depending on his Spirit's leading are essential.

We may be drawn to women who stand out from their peers as we seek leaders in the ministry. Those who are outgoing, winsome, decisive, and have public speaking experience might seem like obvious choices to place into positions of leadership. And if God is so directing, his will will be done, and he will be glorified. But it may very well be that the quiet, hesitant, untrained woman who blends into a crowd is God's person for the job.

Jesus had the weighty task of choosing those who would be with him, learn from him, and lead the way in spreading his fame to the entire world. One would expect him to select high-impact players with impressive résumés, but we know nothing is further from the truth. From an outside view, the most appropriate word to describe Jesus's disciples would be "common." Even though mostly poor, often impulsive, and regularly slow to understand, Jesus's picks were clearly divinely directed. Just prior to calling the Twelve, Jesus "spent all night in prayer to God. When daylight came, he summoned his disciples, and he chose twelve of them, whom he also named apostles" (Luke 6:12–13). Exactly why he chose whom he chose can only be explained by the fact that he was in perfect harmony with his Father and attune to the Spirit's voice. But why did God lead him to these twelve? What were God's criteria and what can we learn from Jesus's method of selection?

A look at the Old Testament may leave us just as baffled at who God placed in positions of leadership. Consistent rebellion and disobedience by God's people resulted in four hundred long and arduous years of their oppression as slaves in Egypt. In his compassion, God ordained that he would provide for their escape and lead them into a land of promise. He could have freed them all with a word. He could have sent a host of angels to destroy their oppressors and carry them to their milk-and-honey destination. But instead, he chose Moses (a hesitant leader, a murderer, adopted and raised in Pharaoh's court) to lead his people and carry out his plan—despite Moses's strong reservations. The Bible records in detail Moses's insistent reluctance in being God's chosen leader in this endeavor. "Who am I that I should go?" he asks God (Exod. 3:11). Then after he follows up his initial question with more pushback expressing his doubts and fears, he concludes with the plea, "Please, Lord, send someone else" (Exod. 4:13). But God stuck by his choice of Moses, gave him a partner for moral and oral support, and accomplished his will. God fulfilled his repeated promise to be with Moses and used him mightily to free the Israelite people, employing some of the most amazing miracles in all of history. God knew something about Moses. He saw something in Moses. Despite Moses's lack of confidence, fear of man, trepidation of public speaking, and occasional outbursts of anger, he was the one. He would listen to God, obey him (mostly), and lead God's people. Most importantly, Moses and God were friends. "The LORD would speak with Moses face to face, just as a man speaks with his friend" (Exod. 33:11).

As we attempt to discern which women God is directing us to invite to take on a leadership role, an honest and humble look at our own lives is the only sage way to begin. We too, in whatever capacity of leadership God has placed us, must recognize our own failings, hesitancies, and shortcomings—in spite of which we have been chosen to fulfill a role in God's kingdom and are impeccably and utterly loved! God knows us perfectly, "remembering that we are dust" (Ps. 103:14). We do well to remember it too! Our hearts are easily deceived, and our motivations readily swayed away from the glory of God to our own desires and personal fame. Knowing that the Lord "will both bring to light what is hidden" and "reveal the intentions of the hearts" (1 Cor. 4:5), the apostle Paul duly reminded the church in Corinth where their gifts, resources, and abilities came from. He did so by asking them this simple rhetorical question: "What do you have that you didn't receive?" (1 Cor. 4:7). All that we have and all that we are is from the abundantly generous hand of God! Therefore, we trust his choice of us and count it a supreme privilege to serve him and invite others to join us in doing so.

Recognizing our lack of foreknowledge, what, in hindsight, can we learn from God's choices and Jesus's selection method? Without the omniscience of God, we won't know all that is in the hearts of the women we are working with, but we do know what God wants to see there because we have seen Jesus's heart. He describes it for us in Matthew 11:

> "Come to me, all of you who are weary and burdened, and I will give you rest. Take my yoke upon you and learn from me, because *I am lowly and humble in heart*, and you will find rest for your souls. For my yoke is easy and my burden is light." (vv. 28–30, emphasis added)

Jesus is unquestionably the greatest and most influential leader of all time, yet his heart is "lowly and humble." As you seek leaders, flashy superstars may attract your attention, but showiness, self-centeredness, superiority, condescension, and pride are all debilitating characteristics in a leader. Look for humble hearts not glitzy stars.

Spending time with a woman in various circumstances will help reveal her character and attitudes. Pray together and open God's Word with her. Ask yourself: Is she teachable? Does she want to know God and be more like him? Does she see her need and admit her weaknesses? Does she sincerely desire to help others grow or merely want the title that comes with a leadership position? Are she and God friends?

Here are few suggestions for discovering the humble hearts God has prepared:

1. Take time alone to seek God's will. If Jesus prayed all night before choosing the twelve, how much more do we need to seek God for his insight? Ask him to recall to your mind interactions you've had and evidences of Christlikeness you've witnessed in the women you are considering. Pray for eyes to see what God sees in the potential leader's life. Seek the guidance of the Holy Spirit. I've often made lists of women's names and prayed over each, asking God to enable me to see them as he does. As I lean toward choosing a particular woman to a leadership role, I seek God to confirm it or show me otherwise. Many times, he's

clearly directed me through a subsequent conversation or circumstance. As you pray over your options, remember that no one is perfect, and God uses broken people like us. As one podcaster so aptly put it, "God has nothing but sinners to work with and he seems to specialize in using the unlikely."[1]

2. Don't rush the process. When in your times of prayer you are left without clarity regarding whom to choose to lead a ministry or program, keep looking and reconsidering. Do you need more information? Is there someone you missed? Only after having exhausted all of Jesse's seven other sons as options was the prophet Samuel led by God to anoint the baby of the family, David, as the future king of Israel. You may not know who God has chosen to lead until you get to know all the women he has placed around you. Some of the most

capable, influential leaders I have had the privilege of working with I almost overlooked. I'm so thankful I took the time to meet them, get to know them, and waited for God to clarify his choice. That said, some of you may be decision averse. If that's you, as you sense God indicating a woman he wants you to ask to step into a leadership role, trust his guidance. Move ahead. Ask him to stop you if you've misunderstood. God wants his will done more than you do and longs for all of us to become ever increasingly familiar with his leading voice.

3. Look for potential. Once you've glimpsed a woman's humble heart, love for God, and desire to serve him, begin to explore her interests and abilities. Don't limit your choice of a leader to one with already developed gifts and skills. Do you see her potential for the role you have in mind? Does she love God's Word

and search it out for truth? You may have found a teacher who needs training. Does she insist on organization and delight in spread sheets? You may have found your long-prayed-for administrator who needs some direction. Does she seek out younger women to encourage and advise? You may have found a mentor who just needs some guidance. Please don't overlook the untrained or inexperienced. We were all there until we weren't! We'll talk more about this in chapter 7.

4. Embrace diversity. There's an easy mistake to make when seeking women to serve and lead alongside you. We tend to gravitate to people just like us— socio-economically, racially, stage of life, personality, interests, and gifts. Yes, we need to be going in the same direction. Yes, we need to have a similar vision and foundation in the gospel. But, as God's

Word clearly states, "Indeed, the body is not one part but many" and if we "were all the same part, where would the body be? As it is, there are many parts, but one body" (1 Cor. 12:14, 19–20). Or, as my former pastor would say, "If two of us agree on everything, one of us is useless!"[2] Our world is vastly varied and within God's united kingdom there is great diversity. Different types of people will reach and appeal to different types of people! We are naturally drawn toward certain personalities or teaching styles over others. A Bible study I coordinated enlisted five separate teachers over the course of its ten weeks. All the teachers were clear, interesting, and handled the text of Scripture carefully. But the personality and individual teaching style of each was evident. Those attending the study all had their favorite, but their choices of "favorite" were equally distributed among the five teachers. God explains the beauty of his plan and the purpose of his design.

> Just as each one has received a gift, use it to serve others, as good stewards of the varied grace of God . . . so that God may be glorified through Jesus Christ in everything. (1 Pet. 4:10–11)

> Now there are different gifts, but the same Spirit. There are different ministries, but the same Lord. And there are different activities, but the same God works all of them in each person. A manifestation of the Spirit is given to each person for the common good. (1 Cor. 12:4–7)

For the beautiful manifestation of the Holy Spirit, the glory of God, and the good of everyone, seek to work with women who are different than you are.

Seek God and take the time necessary to discern in which hearts he is at work. Don't leave out the inexperienced or unlikely. Look for the varied and multifaceted beauty of God in the diversity of his people. Then help guide and develop them into women who know God, are more like him, and are spreading his fame.

REVIEW AND DISCUSS

1. God clearly explains that he looks not at outward appearances in choosing his leaders, but at the heart. What heart characteristics does God highlight as vital? What are your criteria in selecting those with whom you will work?

2. What steps can you take in order to best discern a woman's heart? What circumstances or means might help you see her motives and attitudes?

3. Are you aware of your own strengths, shortcomings, and temperament? Why is it important in choosing co-laborers to recognize your own abilities, weaknesses, and personality

type? Why do you think diversity in the body of Christ is a high value to God?

4. How are you at recognizing potential in others? Are you able to see the unprepared or inexperienced person as someone with great promise given adequate time and training? What are the traits or skills you are looking for which need developing?

CHAPTER 7

How to Polish Developing Stars

*"Those who have insight will shine like the bright
expanse of the heavens, and those who lead many to
righteousness, like the stars forever and ever."*
(Dan. 12:3)

THERE ARE FEW, IF any, superstars on God's roster. More often
than not, he chooses inexperienced and seemingly unprepared
people to further his kingdom work. But he doesn't leave
them there. God instructs and refines those who are his for
his purposes. He goes before them and with them, leading,
guiding, coaching, and teaching. As God gives us the great
privilege of working alongside women to help them grow
spiritually, he wants to use us to develop them into leaders,
teachers, and guides of others.

How do we take the women he has chosen, nurture their God-focused hearts, and help them mature into the kind of stars who "lead many to righteousness" (Dan. 12:3)? There is a process which God uses to polish his developing stars, clearly demonstrated in the life of Jesus.

Jesus related with his followers as their friend and rabbi. And as their rabbi, his task was to ready them for their future roles as leaders in his kingdom. Throughout the Gospels, we see Jesus preparing his disciples. He was their constant model in word and deed. He was their teacher and trainer, giving explanations and instructions in what to do and how to do it. He provided opportunities for his followers to put into practice what they were learning. He followed up their experiences with debrief and feedback, and then gave them additional opportunities.

The women that we are helping to grow will benefit greatly from this same approach. An essential component often missing in our churches is that of adequately preparing our people. We invite a person to fulfill a role and see how she does. If she does a good job, we've discovered our next teacher or emcee or event organizer. But if she fails, not meeting our standards, we don't ask her again. We haven't found the person we're looking for, and the woman who gave it a try is now sidelined with "failure" written across her forehead. Lose. Lose.

Instead, we can follow Jesus's method. He calls on us to 1) model character and skills, 2) supply needed practical training, 3) provide hands-on opportunities, 4) give feedback, and 5) then provide more opportunities.

FOLLOW JESUS'S METHOD

Modeling

God's divine task in women's lives starts with his work in your own life. You may be the only up close and personal, flesh-and-blood model this woman has as she learns how to grow in godliness and lead others humbly. What you do and how you do it will be the example after which she and others will pattern themselves. That's intimidating . . . Focusing on all the possible mistakes you may make, and all your sinful tendencies won't help. What *will* help is keeping your eyes on Jesus, taking your cues from him, and moment by moment increasing your dependence on him. Then keep showing her how to do that!

If you are operating out of a humble heart, seeking to glorify God, depending on his Spirit, and wanting to be used by him for the good of others, it will not go unnoticed by the women around you. Then, inevitably, when your character or behavior falls miserably short of your Savior's, confess it and point women back to him (1 John 1:9).

As you strive to help a woman develop her skills in a particular area, do your best to model, rather than simply explain, how to accomplish it. Show and tell, don't just tell. Show her how to spend alone time with God if it's new to her. Do a Bible study *with* her rather than simply explaining a method. Call her alongside you as you spread the fame of God. If you are helping her develop her teaching skills, give her ample opportunities to listen to you, or to other recommended teachers, who do it well. Be the leader you want her to be. Lead her like you want her to lead others.

Training

God's Word is replete with synonyms for *train*: teach, correct, instruct, warn, prepare, and discipline, to name a few. We are called on not to leave others uneducated in the knowledge of God nor ill-equipped in using their God-given gifts. Learning and growing are an essential part of life and are indispensable in our development in Christlikeness. We must take advantage of every opportunity to provide others with instruction on how to carry out responsibilities and how to improve in the use of their gifts.

Soon after we began a women's Bible study at our church, we felt the weight of having too many chapters to cover and not enough women trained to teach them. Our clear desire was for all the women to know God and learn from those who are "correctly teaching the word of truth" (2 Tim. 2:15). Following the outstanding model of "Charles Simeon Trust Workshops,"[1] we offered "Teacher Development Training." It was a four-week course for any woman who wanted to grow in her ability to study and teach God's Word. We had women interested in learning to teach in our Bible study, in our student ministry, in our kids' ministry, and others who simply wanted to teach their own kids and neighbors. We took them through passages of Scripture, providing them with detailed steps to uncover the author's meaning, to see the beauty of the gospel, and to present their findings in a way that was persuasive and applicable. As they learned, they put every step into practice, culminating with a ten-minute message in front of three or four of their peers. As we leaders listened, we were repeatedly astounded by the excellence in their talks. To a woman, the training proved beneficial. To some, it unveiled a gift for teaching God's Word and provided the preparedness to do so. (Appendix 6 contains a brief outline for our Teacher Development Training and Criteria for the participants ten-minute talks.)

For every need that exists, there is a right person to fill it. It's possible however, that the right person isn't quite ready. She needs to be trained. Teach her to teach. Train her in giving counsel. Instruct her in leadership skills. Prepare her to mentor others. Then you must provide her with opportunities to use her gift and skills.

Hands-On Ministry Opportunities

Once you see women trained and eager, opening up hands-on opportunities for them to use their gifts is vitally important. It may mean you need to step away from the podium so that a first-timer can try her skills. Or it may mean you need to create a new ministry program just to give women a chance to hone their gifts. Whatever it looks like, providing outlets for women to gain experience and grow from that experience is a necessary step in their development.

Many women who completed our teacher training course showed interest and ability in teaching the Bible but needed more experience. From this need, "James in 15" was born. We divided the book of James into twelve short sections and recruited twelve training course "graduates" to teach each section. We explained our expectations clearly and thoroughly. We talked through their outlines with them. We addressed any difficulties they were having. And we gave them input and suggestions. Then the women recorded their fifteen-minute lessons on their phones, and we posted them on our church's women's private Facebook page. Throughout the summer, women from our church listened and learned from the book of James. It took organization, instruction, and coaching. The new teachers were sometimes nervous, frequently did retakes, but always, without exception, thanked us for the opportunity they had to grow. (For James in 15 ideas, see Appendix 6).

On a different occasion, a women's ministry intern came to me with a need to grow in her teaching experience before she went out onto the mission field. At the time, there were no such opportunities available at our church, so together we created a women's discipleship course. My intern helped me design the syllabus and taught four out of the six lessons. Those who attended the class certainly benefitted, but the primary beneficiaries were the intern and those ultimately touched by a missionary to Central America who grew in her teaching ability.

Feedback

Even if we are committed to training through modeling, giving instruction, and providing opportunities to practice and hone new skills, we frequently still have a missing component. It's the feedback piece. Particularly in working with Christian women, there is a tendency to only offer praise for their service—omitting correction or anything that would hint at negativity. We want to encourage, thinking that encouragement means helping people feel better. But true encouragement helps people *be* better. It's possible to offer suggestions for improvement in a way that not only doesn't offend a woman's feelings but actually inspires her and builds her up.

We made a commitment to provide feedback to each of our Bible study teachers immediately following her lesson. While she taught, another leader and I took copious notes using the teaching guidelines all our teachers were instructed to follow. We then spent forty minutes focused on the teacher and her message. This time of debriefing became a highlight for all of us. It gave us, as leaders, the opportunity to commend the women for their investment of time and effort and to share with them how God used them in our lives to communicate his character and truth. It provided the teachers with immediate feedback and appreciation for their hard work. As we walked through their messages, we had countless good things to say! And each teacher knew going in that we would discuss one or two items that could make her content, structure, or delivery stronger. How we addressed them made all the difference. Rather than underscoring the weaknesses in her teaching, we always expressed our thoughts as suggestions for improvement. For example, if a talk was longer than the allotted time, instead of saying, "Your teaching was too long," we would have ready a suggestion to trim her message to be more pointed and powerful. Or if she had a distracting habit, like swaying as she spoke, we would emphasize the strength of her message and give her ideas to use her body language to add to, rather than take away from, her content. If we were confused by a point she was making, we would ask her to explain it to us and then rework the wording together to clarify it.

"Feedback time" became for all of us—regardless of our level of experience—immensely profitable and rewarding as we all grew to be more effective in our teaching.

In whatever area of ministry a woman is serving, show her, through providing individual attention and gracious suggestions for improvement, that you are committed to helping her grow. She will thank you for it.

Opportunities 2.0

Giving a woman who is growing spiritually a first opportunity to use her gifts and try her skills is empowering and motivating. Not offering her subsequent opportunities is disheartening and discouraging. Progress requires practice. When a woman is being trained and is investing her time to develop her gifts, sidelining her—even unintentionally—is not an option. If she needs more "polishing," provide occasions for her to do that. If she is operating outside of her gifting and needs to be redirected to another area of service, speak the truth in love and help redirect her. Remember that the goal is to help form strong women who "lead many to righteousness," so finding good and right places for these stars to shine is vital.

It is easy as leaders with full plates and busy lives to lose track of who has done what, and where individual women are in their "star polishing" journey. One significant take-away from my experience as a women's director was how I often fell short in record-keeping. Lists of women's names who have participated, notes about their gifts, strengths, and needs, and accounts of conversations with them may feel like necessary evils, but they are great allies. Each name is a person who God is growing into his likeness. She may be looking to you for the next "ask," waiting to put her newly developed skills into practice. Very literally, by "taking note" of people, it will help you to see their potential, interests, areas to grow, and progress.

Polishing takes time, effort, patience, and proximity. Think about your people. Pray for your people. Be a model of ministry skills and God's character to them. Train them. Provide opportunities for them to put their training into practice. Give them constructive feedback. Then continue providing them with more opportunities. God is using you to spread his fame, and your insight in doing so "will shine like the bright expanse of the heavens" (Dan. 12:3).

REVIEW AND DISCUSS

1. Do you see yourself as a model for others in their growth towards Christlikeness? What characteristics and habits can you cultivate to help you be a better, more helpful example?

2. Why do you think providing training for women in Christian growth and the use of spiritual gifts is essential in the life of a church? What are the results when it is absent? What might it look like in your context?

3. Openings for "apprentice stars" to have opportunities to hone their teaching and leading skills are often lacking in

our churches. A few established leaders frequently lead while the rest sit on the sidelines. How might you create a variety of occasions for trained women to use their gifts and "polish" their abilities?

4. Why is feedback so important for our development? How can you cultivate your ability to give and receive constructive feedback and demonstrate a commitment to mutual growth in the body of Christ?

CHAPTER 8

How to Cultivate Healthy Hearts

YOU AND I ARE quite literally on the same page. We've made it to chapter 8 and we are committed to helping women grow. We want to glorify God in our lives and see him glorified in the women we invest in. We want them to know God, become more like him, and make him famous. By now you've probably taken more than one look at the Appendices and are coming up with ideas and plans. But there's a danger in doing women's ministry, and that's overdoing it.

The work of building into two, two hundred, or two thousand others doesn't attract underachievers. We are much more likely to live a hurried life and keep a schedule of diminishing margins. It is vital then that we listen as Jesus teaches us his designs for our time, for our lives, and for our ministry.

Just before he discloses his heart as "lowly and humble," Jesus invites all who are weary and burdened to come to him

(Matt. 11:28–30). That pretty much describes each of us at any given time: weary and burdened. Regardless of our spiritual state or the vibrancy of our vision, ministry is challenging, and life is hard. The fears, frustrations, setbacks, and struggles we all face stir up worry and anxiety in the healthiest of hearts. So Jesus, knowing what we need, calls us to himself to find refreshment. Jesus's solution is not for us to run around trying to find fixes, but for us to come to him. He points us to the Father who made us, loves us, and keeps us. Our trust in God, his works, and his ways is the only remedy for weary hearts. It's essential then, that we never forget who he is, what he's done, and how to find rest.

REMEMBERING

God has shown us his lavish love and his unfailing faithfulness. He has done great, miraculous things for us. He has given us sure, incredible promises. What he asks of us—over and over and over again—is that we remember.

When challenges come, we take our eyes off God's character and his past faithfulness, leaving us fearful, anxious, or worried. Jesus's own disciples witnessed him miraculously heal the mute, the crippled, the lame, and the blind (Matt. 15:31). They assisted as their Lord multiplied loaves and fish to feed hungry crowds of over five thousand, then more than four thousand. Yet, soon after, when a discussion arose among the twelve because they were without bread, Jesus implored them: "You of little faith, why are you discussing among yourselves that you do not have bread? Don't you understand yet? Don't you remember the five loaves for the five thousand and how many baskets you collected? Or the seven loaves for the four thousand and how many large baskets you collected?" (Matt. 16:8–10). God is our provider, and he provides. But we forget that.

Throughout the Old Testament, God's people were repeatedly told to "remember the wondrous works he has done, his wonders, and the judgments he has pronounced" (Ps. 105:5). And they were commanded to "remember his covenant forever—the promise he ordained for a thousand generations" (1 Chron. 16:15). King David even charged his own soul with remembering: "My soul, bless the LORD, and do not forget all his benefits" (Ps. 103:2). We are begged to remember because we are so prone to forget!

After having followed God for forty years in the wilderness, only the flooded Jordan River stood between tens of thousands of weary Israelites and their promised land. In obedience to God's command, the priests carrying the ark of the covenant stepped foot into the Jordan, "and the water flowing downstream stood still, rising up in a mass" (Josh. 3:16). Then the priests "stood firmly on dry ground in the middle of the Jordan, while all Israel crossed on dry ground until the entire nation had finished crossing the Jordan" (v. 17).

Men, women, and children witnessed and experienced an unforgettable miracle! Who would have predicted, then, that immediately after the last person passed over the dry riverbed, God would command twelve of the leaders to go right back to the middle of the river. He sent them to gather twelve large "souvenir" stones. Those stones were to be visible reminders to them of God's power, provision, and promise-keeping for all the future generations—just in the likely case that they'd forget.

God is also very mindful of *our* forgetfulness and knows that it is essential that we remember. He did the impossible in our lives. He took our sins and gave us his righteousness through Jesus's unforgettable death on the cross. He paid for us to draw near to him and dwell with him forever. Then he commanded us to have tangible reminders of broken bread and poured-out wine so that we'd never forget (1 Cor. 11:23–26).

Day-to-day ministry activities and busy schedules can cloud our memories of God's incredible goodness, what he has done, and what he is currently doing in our midst. Forgetfulness depletes our spiritual resources and diminishes our faith. We will go a long way in nourishing the hearts of our leaders and our own hearts if we encourage and establish habits of remembering.

- Practice thankfulness. Rehearse God's good character and share glimpses of his kindness with the women you are discipling. Before you move on to the next event or program, remember and give thanks for the last one. Thank God for what he did and thank the women who helped make it happen. Share stories of the big and little ways he was at work. Taking time for grateful remembering should not be an optional "extra" in our lives and ministries. Making it a habit

will cultivate in all of us a proper focus
and a right attitude.

- Keep a journal. Record answers to
  prayer, needs supplied, acts of faithfulness of God, and evidences of his grace
  in your life. Then share your entries with
  the women around you. We face the
  future with greater faith and confidence
  when we can recall God's trustworthy
  acts in the past. Some of the most valuable times with my leaders were those in
  which I passed on what God was doing
  in my life and how he was revealing
  himself to me.

- Gather up "souvenir stones," and put
  them in a central place where all can see.
  They might be photos, physical reminders, or actual commemorative rocks with
  dates and notations regarding acts of
  God. Then keep the memories fresh by
  regularly reviewing with your leaders,
  your friends, your family, (and strangers)

the stories of God's faithfulness which the rocks represent.

- Celebrate! The Old Testament records God's numerous commands for his people to celebrate his character and his works through festivals and feasts (Lev. 23). His people were to "Rejoice before the Lord your God" (Deut. 16:11). It took getting to know Jesus in real time for me to understand that he is full of vibrant, jubilant life. (Too many movie depictions and oil paintings had previously convinced me otherwise.) Hosting a women's event for the sole purpose of celebrating Jesus with joyful worship, meaningful symbols of his work in our lives, and delicious food would bring glory to him and nourish many hearts—and stomachs.

- Worship. You may be tempted to set up meetings with women during the Sunday worship gathering while you are all in one place. Or you may feel the need to skip the service to retreat to a back room to do last-minute prep while the kids are being taken care of. Resist. Prioritizing the worship of God with other believers is foundational to our spiritual well-being. When we worship, we are acknowledging who God is and that he is worthy to be praised. We rehearse his greatness, his goodness, and his "otherness." We consider his works in the past and his faithfulness in the present. Through corporate singing and prayer, the teaching of God's Word, and participation in the Lord's Supper, our hearts, souls, minds, and bodies are engaged in reminders of who we love, what he has done, and how he loves us.

Remembering God in all his good and great perfections is an invaluable privilege and will help make us that much more eager and hopeful to draw near to him for comfort, healing, and rest.

RESTING

From week one of planet earth, God established a "rest period" (Gen. 2:2–3). He did his creative work in six days; then he rested. When he gave the Law to Moses, he commanded that his people rest (Exod. 31:12–17). As newly freed slaves under harsh Egyptian rule, the Israelites must have found this as astonishing as it was wonderful! Their God didn't want them to work 24/7, always doing, always serving, always producing. They were to do their best work in six days, then, as he had done, stop, and rest.

God introduced this regular rhythm to his people with this explanation: "you must observe my Sabbaths . . . so that you will know that I am the LORD who consecrates you" (Exod. 31:13). Resting from their labors would not only bring welcome relief to their bodies and minds, but it would also serve as a clear indicator that working more or working harder didn't and couldn't affect their status before God. To consecrate means to set apart or to make holy for special purposes. Their work didn't set them apart. Nothing they did could make them righteous or more special to God. It wasn't their efforts that made them accepted by God and invited into his presence. It was the Lord who had chosen them, and he was pleased with the work that he was doing in them to set them apart.

Resting is a lovely portrait of God's beautiful gospel. When we rest, we are reminded that our value to God and our future with him are not dependent upon or because of the work that we do. Jesus did the work, completing all that God required on our behalf through his sinless life and his death on the cross. As Jesus breathed his last, he said, "It is finished," and he meant it (John 19:30). No more ceaseless striving to make ourselves worthy of God's presence. Jesus did everything necessary to ensure our entrance into God's place of forever, celebratory, perfect rest. As we learn to put aside our need to do it all and fix it all, all the time, we give public acknowledgment to the truth that this is God's world, not ours, and he can be trusted to take care of it. And we show ourselves and those around us that we belong to him, and we trust him to take care of us.

In your ministry alongside women, you communicate the truth and validity of the gospel and the generous provisions of God when you accept Jesus's invitation to rest and when you extend that invitation to others.

- Talk to women about God's intentions when he instituted the Sabbath. Explain that it's not just about pacing ourselves. It's about letting God set the pace and trusting him to go slower or faster as he sees fit. Teach them that constant work or always doing more is not God's plan, but on the contrary, actually demonstrates a lack of trust in his ability to provide for us. Resting reveals our belief that God can and has done it all with nothing whatsoever from us.

- Rest in your place in God's big story. The universe is dependent on God, not you, and it's in good hands. He's the sovereign king and he will carry out his purposes. Walk in the Spirit. Obey God's leading. Do your best work. Then rest. As my son would often tell me, "Mom, you're only indispensable until you say 'no.'"

- Introduce women to the Jesus who models for us not only purposeful work and self-sacrifice, but also creativity, vibrancy, joy, and rest. Show them the God-man who clearly understood his priorities. He unhurriedly finished every bit of his Father's will, told ingenious stories, spent significant getaways in prayer, took time for feasting and celebrating, and slept.

- Advise women to say "no"—guilt free—to "one more thing" when their plates are already too full. Recognize that some of the women you're working with will have only "yes" in their vocabulary. They want to please. They want to serve. They will do whatever you ask, often at the expense of their own well-being or the good of their families. Model rest and teach them priorities. And then be sure to show them lavish grace when they finally say "no" and it happens to be to a ministry request from you!

- Involve more women. Women's ministry exists to provide teaching, training, hope, fellowship, and serving opportunities for all the women in the church. It is too easy, as we lead, to continue to call on the same faithful few. After all, they are faithful, and you have their numbers on speed dial. But God has gifted all the women and has gone ahead of each and prepared good works for them to do (Eph. 2:10). Always be on the lookout for new or uninvolved faces. Invite them to serve and encourage your faithful few to take time to rest.

- Subtraction is good too. We have a tendency to add more and more and more events and plans until the yoke of them is burdensome and their value is lost. Be at peace with discontinuing a program—or two or three—in favor of doing that which better serves your desired ends. God's people are sacred; our programs are not.

- Communicate regularly that God (and you) love the women you are working with for who they are, not what they do. They are beloved of God when they are fully engaged in serving and when they are not. Their value is not in their role, but in their identity as image-bearers and in their relationship to their King.

- Spread out events and programs as you plan your ministry calendar, choosing dates and times which minimize stress in an already demanding world. Be mindful of maintaining a rhythm of work and rest. We had a lot of families with school-aged children, so we always planned our women's schedule with the church and school calendars in hand. Predictably we began our fall Bible study after Labor Day and ended it before Thanksgiving.

- Watch your programming around major holidays. Christmas can be stressful enough all by itself. Find ways to simplify while still accomplishing your desired outcomes. Remember it's people over programs. And people need rest. We had an annual Christmas women's event which set the tone for the season. It was very enjoyable, included much interaction time, filled everyone's stomachs with brunch foods, sent all home with gifts, provided an opportunity to give to a special need, and focused our attention on the Savior whose birthday we were celebrating. We intentionally scheduled it for the first Saturday in December (before things got out-of-control busy), followed the same much-loved program each year (which significantly streamlined our planning), and spread out the workload among many women (lightening everyone's load).

- Meet with women you are working alongside to talk about life, to laugh, and to pray, not only to discuss the next ministry project. You are journeying together to know God, see him change you, and make him famous. Notice his image reflected in others' lives and listen to his voice speaking through sisters in Christ. Learn to find the joy and rest he longs to provide in the relationships he has given you.

- Provide an end date when you recruit women for ministry roles. Then hold to it. Remember (and remind them) that there are seasons in life and that neither stepping into or out of a ministry assignment is a lifelong commitment. Encourage people to serve and encourage them to take breaks from serving. A scheduled "finish line" for rest motivates us to work hard and then rest in preparation for future opportunities.

- Whenever possible, take your meetings outside. Go for a walk. Sit under a tree. Consider the birds and observe how the wildflowers grow, remembering who made them and who gives them everything they need (Matt. 6:28–30). We can find rest in creation because we can see God in his handiwork. The heavens declare his glory (Ps. 19:1) and he has made his invisible attributes visible and understandable to us in the things that he has made (Rom. 1:20). Seeing his incredible workmanship and his providential care over all that he has made reminds us of what he is like and what he is capable of doing in our lives. We can release our anxiety, breathe, and rest because God is God, and he takes care of us.

- Listen to your own needs and those of your leaders. If you need a change of pace in the summer, chances are the women around you do as well. If you are feeling weary from a particularly trying season, do for others what you would love to have done for you. As our area of the country crawled out of the pandemic, most of the women in our church were worn down from Zoom meetings, social distancing, isolation, and schooling at home. We were in need of fellowship and refreshment. What I personally longed for was to have my favorite Christian female artist sing God's words over me. After a bit of planning and chair arranging, the women were blessed to see other's faces (albeit masked ones) and hear a gifted, godly singer-songwriter remind us of the grace and mercy, and the goodness and beauty of God. Afterward, many women commented to me how restorative, restful, and needed the time was for them personally. But none was more grateful for that rest and refreshment from God than I.

All we have—our time, our families and friends, our ministry opportunities, our occupations, and our resources—is a gift. We steward that gift as best as we know how and then we rest, trusting that the Giver has the whole world in his hands, he knows what he's doing, and he's very good.

In Jesus, we are promised not just life, but life in abundance (John 10:10). He will cultivate in us full, strong, satisfied, healthy hearts as we employ the means he supplies. He bids us to a life of remembering and calls us to rhythms of rest in him.

REVIEW AND DISCUSS

1. Remembering the character and work of our God is foundational for our spiritual health. What habits are you practicing to help you know and remember what God is like and what he has done? Are there tangible reminders you could use to commemorate God's intervention(s) in your life?

2. What is the "rest" which God instituted a portrayal of? Why is recognizing God's purpose for and meaning behind a day of rest important for us today?

3. Our tendency in doing "God's work" is to constantly add more to our schedules in an effort to please him. Instead, have you considered what plans or programs God might want you to eliminate from your calendar in order to enjoy him and have more unhurried time for people?

4. How do the practices of remembering and resting aid us in knowing God, becoming more like him, and spreading his fame?

CHAPTER 9

Teamwork: Keeping Hearts and Stars Aligned

"If you want to go fast go alone.
If you want to go far, go together."
(African proverb)

BECAUSE THE SINGULAR PRONOUN "you" in English is indistinguishable from the plural "you," we often miss the fact that God is directing his commands, instructions, and promises to more than just one of us. He regularly speaks to us in the plural. He teaches a community of believers to pray to "our" Father (Matt. 6:9). He compares the church to a multi-membered body (1 Cor. 12:12–14), a building composed of many and various living stones (1 Pet. 2:4–5), and a family made up males and females spanning the generations (1 Tim. 3:14–15; 5:1–2). Never did God intend for us to go it alone, in life or in ministry. We are to work and grow together—diverse players on a unified team—supporting and strengthening one another.

Teamwork, then, plays a central role in our work of leading and discipling women. We can have great ideas and many skills, but unless we learn to effectively facilitate collaboration with others, we may go fast, but we won't go far. Teamwork means that diverse individuals share an objective and put the goals of the team ahead of their own. It's a collective of distinct persons who, in an environment of trust and support, act together to move the group forward for the benefit of all.

A beautiful and yet sometimes challenging aspect of ministry teams is that they are alive and growing, never static. I've read that when decorating a room, house plants are a great addition—and designer gurus always recommend using only real, living ones, not silk or plastic. But, oh, how tempting the fake ones are! They stay the same size and shape, and don't need any care. You can put them wherever you want them and forget about them. Teams of living people (the best kind to work with), have their own opinions, are always changing, and need frequent care. The approach you use to deal with one person successfully may fall flat with her sister in Christ.

Two women you love and with whom you are eager to serve may rub each other the wrong way. A group of six women will have six different ideas and each is sure that hers is the best one. Your job is to put your various people in the right places, take good care of them, and keep making adjustments as they grow individually and collectively toward God's goals for them. Some developing superstar plants will need pruning, so they don't take over. Some fragile-hearted seedlings will need more light and extra nourishment. You will need the Spirit of God and all the wisdom he provides.

You will likely require two different types of teams as you work to accomplish God's purposes: 1) A leadership team, made up of those women who will have a major role in influencing the direction of the ministry and shepherding others and 2) Serving teams which will help to execute events or classes in more limited, short-term capacities. Many of the principles below pertain to both types of teams, however, keep in mind the different expectations of the various roles, as you read through them. Your leadership team will set the pace, help you determine the direction, hold you accountable, and model for others. You will be looking for other specific skills and abilities in the women who make up the temporary serving teams. Learning to recruit for those jobs will be helpful to you. More on building these serving teams can be found at the end of this chapter.

FORMING LEADERSHIP TEAMS

Your task is to help women grow in their knowledge of God, their likeness to him, and their spreading of his fame. You will find that as you do so, you will need to recruit others who will work with you to move the mission forward. It will be your job to discern who God has chosen to lead alongside you, draw them together into a team, and provide the ongoing care and input they will need. There are no foolproof, one, two, three steps to make this happen, but some sound principles are a big help.

Pray

The first (and continual) step in discerning who your leaders will be is to pray. God gives us a sobering warning through the prophet Isaiah.

> Woe to the rebellious children!
> This is the LORD's declaration.

> They carry out a plan, but not mine;
> they make an alliance,
> but against my will,
> piling sin on top of sin.
> Without asking my advice
> they set out to go down to Egypt
> in order to seek shelter under Pharaoh's protection
> and take refuge in Egypt's shadow. (Isa. 30:1–2)

How easy it is to carry out our own plans and move forward with our decisions without asking God's advice! He has already done the choosing of our co-laborers (John 15:16). We simply need to ask him to lead us to our teammates and to prepare them to say yes. Will we sometimes get it wrong or misunderstand? Of course. But does he want to lead us clearly to do his will? Absolutely. He tells us to ask, seek, and knock in order to receive, find, and discover open doors (Matt. 7:7–8). Our heavenly Father loves to give us good things and guide us by his Spirit (Matt. 7:11; Luke 11:13).

Choosing the Right People

Without a doubt, as you seek women to work and lead alongside you, you are first looking for those with godly character. The prophet Micah beautifully summarizes God's requirements of his followers: "Mankind, he has told each of you what is good and what it is the LORD requires of you: to act justly, to love faithfulness, and to walk humbly with your God" (Mic. 6:8). Fair and righteous behaviors, truthful and dependable hearts, and modest and humble attitudes are qualities to seek in the women around you. None of us has arrived, but as we observe a woman growing in these characteristics of Christlikeness, we will want to ask God if she is his choice to lead other women.

Depending on the ministry role and responsibility, you will be searching out other suitable characteristics. For example, if you are in need of a woman to lead middle and high school girls, you will likely want to put "flexible," "patient," and "relates well with young people" on your list of criteria. On the other hand, if you're looking for a woman to be the administrator for your ministry, "detail oriented," "technical skills," and "punctual" may make your list. This is important as you might find a woman of great character and commitment to God and yet discover that she is unsuitable for her role. If her gifts and personality don't fit the responsibilities of a particular position, both the leader and those she's serving will suffer. As you recruit women, have a clear picture in your own mind of the type of person who is most likely to enjoy and find success doing certain tasks or dealing with specific people.

Knowing that a woman at our church was faithful to God and had a great vision for women's ministry, I began giving her more and more responsibility in organizing our events. It wasn't long before I saw the stressed and beleaguered look on her face. She found having to think through details and manage time schedules draining and unfulfilling. Moving her "up" in event organizing and execution was a bad decision on my part. After just a ninety-minute coffee date with her, I saw what I had missed. She had a wonderful vision. She was exploding with good ideas. She was in touch with the needs of women. And she was overwhelmed by details. I immediately removed her from the organization/execution side of our planning, and instead, she became one of my foremost go-to idea persons. From that point on, I'd often get praise for the creative and clever ways we were building up women and meeting their needs. And my response would usually be: "That was Ashley's idea."

We will all probably serve in areas that are outside of our gifting from time to time. We will see a need and help to fill it. We will likely ask others to do the same. God will honor that. But this is not where we need to stay. It's not how we want to manage the gifts that God has put under our care. It's not how we want to go about appointing leaders. A wise pastor I served with relayed to our staff team the words Jesus spoke to his disciples at a well in Samaria. When they expressed concern that Jesus hadn't eaten, he replied, "My food is to do the will of him who sent me and to finish his work" (John 4:34). My pastor then added, "And his will and his work shouldn't give us indigestion!" If you are finding that women on your team are experiencing ministry indigestion, you may need to help them by changing their diet.

Clarifying Your Expectations

When asking a woman to take on a particular role or additional responsibilities, clarity is key. Write out a job description. It doesn't have to be elaborate or formal, but it should clearly explain what you expect of the woman taking on this role. In it, include:

- The goal of the project or ministry, front and center. You and she will need to return to this often and refer to it every time plans are being made. Losing sight of the purpose of the ministry is a sure-fire way to discouragement and failure.

- A list of the responsibilities of the person stepping into this role. This list is absolutely necessary for a woman to see what she is saying yes or no to. And writing it out will be a huge help for you as well. It will simplify in your mind what the role requires and the qualities and capabilities you are looking for to fill it.

- The names of the people this woman would be responsible for and to. If she will inherit a team or need to form her own team to help her, let her know that up front. And be sure to tell her who she reports to. Questions in all our minds when taking on a new role are, "Who will care for me?," "Who will I work with?," and "Who do I go to with problems or questions?"

- A beginning and ending date. Many of us already have plans on the calendar for a year out. In order for a woman to evaluate her ability to say yes to a new role, she must know how it fits into the bigger picture of her life. It is to everyone's advantage to have a date set when a commitment ends. It will help her jump in with both feet, push to the finish line, and then rest. And if, for any reason, a woman is not the best fit for a particular role, you will be glad that she won't be expecting to fill that role indefinitely.

- An average weekly and/or monthly time commitment. Much like the starting and ending date, clarifying the expected investment of time in the ministry enables women to judge whether or not this type of service is reasonable for them. Be sure not to underestimate the time commitment and be open to negotiations. You will lose people midstream if your demands far exceed their expectations and limits. And if the number of hours is too great for the woman you're asking, you may be able to divide up responsibilities and let another woman share the load.

Communicating the Upside

As you propose a new leadership responsibility to a woman you've been led by God to recruit, share the upside of being a part of your team. This pre-supposes that there are upsides! Your team should be a place where the women see God at work, their gifts are developed, they become more like him, and relationships go deeper. The women God has chosen will want to be a part of this! Many of these "intangibles" are exactly what women are longing for and often missing in ministry. Thus, as you share the job responsibilities, be sure to include the benefits to the new leader.

Celebrating Her Response

You have prayed, thought through character qualities, laid out a job description, shared the upsides, and asked a woman to join your leadership team. Now you need to wait. Give her time to think and pray before she responds. *Insist* that she takes time before she responds! She needs to look at her other commitments. She needs to evaluate how this will impact her family or other relationships. She needs to pray and see if this is the direction God is leading her. Suggest a date to reconnect and get her answer. A week is usually a good amount of time.

Then celebrate her response. If it's a yes, express your joy in having her be a part of the team. Be sure to have a next step ready and share it with her. It may be a follow-up call with information or a first meeting date with the team. She has considered this and prayed and moved forward. It's important now to draw her in and give her a vision for what's coming.

If her response is a no, express your sincere appreciation for her consideration of your offer. God is putting your team together and through her "no" is revealing his direction to both of you. That's also something to find joy in. Make sure, then, that you understand what her no means. Is it no to this responsibility because she is interested in becoming involved another way? Is it no for now, with an openness to serve at a later time? Is it a Moses kind of no because of feelings of inadequacy? Her explanation will help you know her and clarify her future involvement for both of you.

FORMING SERVICE TEAMS

As opportunities to serve more women arise, you will want to invite a variety of women to take on more limited roles in order to carry out specific ministry initiatives. For these, sharpening your ability to identify and recruit women who suit the job and assigning those jobs to suit the women will be extremely helpful to you. You will likely be looking for servants for childcare, hospitality, event registration, printing needs, emcees, and much more. I wish I had learned earlier how to think about and explain my needs as I recruited women. I had previously looked to fill positions. I needed a "childcare coordinator," or a "hospitality lead." I finally discovered that instead, I should recruit in terms of the personal qualities the role required, not the position's title. Rather than looking for a childcare coordinator, I needed to seek out a woman who loved children, had a vision for and the skills to share God's Word with little ones, and could recruit others to help her. And likewise, rather than looking for a head of hospitality, I needed a woman who demonstrated hospitality herself, was able to anticipate others' needs, and could, with the help of others, create a welcoming atmosphere to all who attended our events. It was a reordering of the horse before the cart for me. Focusing my attention on the qualities I wanted to find enabled me to look for and ask the right people. I could then share with the women I selected the reason I chose them, and they could see that they were indeed a good fit. They had all the prerequisite skills, personality, and gifting for the role.

Although this team is limited in scope for the duration of an event or program, the "personal principle" still applies. When proposing a ministry opportunity to a woman, do so face to face. You are recruiting a person, so ask her in person. Nothing causes burn-out and discouragement in ministry faster than treating those who serve as "slot-fillers" rather than family members and friends. Even if you have given in to the temptation to broadcast your need for workers on Facebook (guilty as charged!), when it comes to following up with any who respond, look them in the eyes. It will only take a minute, maybe three, to talk personally at church, but the benefits are huge. You will be getting to know them, and they will feel known.

At a former church I attended, I responded favorably to a Facebook plea to join a team of emcees for women's programs and events. I then began receiving, every other month or so, a form e-mail explaining my "script." I provided my automated yes or no response and to every yes, I showed up, did the introductions and announcements I had been told. It was a "slot" I enjoyed filling, but I must admit, it felt a bit dehumanizing. No one spoke to me about it, gave me feedback, or thanked me. I simply waited for my next form email to arrive and filled the slot. The family of God is not anything if it is not personal. No matter the role we are seeking to fill, let's make sure to keep it personal.

Planning Your Meetings

Once you get a group of women around you, whether it is your leadership team or a short-term planning committee for an event, you will have to meet. Meetings are necessary, but they don't have to be a necessary evil. I know you've attended bad meetings. Maybe you've even led bad meetings! What were their downsides? Were they too long? Boring? Irrelevant? Don't have that kind. Remember that the focus of your ministry is people, so the focus of your ministry meetings should be people—the people at the meeting and the people you will be ministering to because of your meeting. Some suggestions that may help:

- Pray and decide what those on your team need to know, to feel, and to do. Are they discouraged and needing to be reminded of what God is doing in and through them? Do they need to be thanked and given gestures of appreciation? Are they ready to be challenged, take on greater responsibility, and needing to know next steps? Likewise, determine at the outset what those for whom this team exists need to know, feel, and do. What should the mood and atmosphere of the event or class you are planning be? What is the bottom-line goal you are wanting to achieve? Keep it clear and simple. You may need to remind the team of the goal often as you go hopping down rabbit trails.

- Think through what decisions must be made at this meeting, what assignments must be delegated, and what can wait. Cover topics that are of relevance to all and be diligent to reach the conclusions that need to be reached. I've led meetings with a lot of great conversation but left important details undecided upon. Oops.

- Start and end your meetings on time. Women's time is valuable and should be respected.

- Write out an agenda with the topics to be covered and give everyone a copy. Order your agenda starting with the most important, must-make decisions, and move on from there. By putting first things first, you are communicating to your team what your priorities are, getting their input on the most significant ones when they are fresh, and making sure the critical items to be covered don't get crowded out by the less important ones.

- If you are leading the meeting, make sure someone besides yourself is writing down what's being decided, who's volunteering to do what, and what you are committing to! It's too easy, once you've reached number seven on the agenda, to forget what details you said you'd take care of on number three. I put a big star on my notes next to any commitments I make as we go through our planning meetings and then I still check with the woman also taking notes to see what I missed.

- Rabbit trails are in abundance at planning meetings. Your agenda will help. Keep referring to it and summarize each item's decisions as you move on to the next. If a team member is in charge of table decorations, remember that *she is* in charge of table decorations. Please don't spend twenty precious meeting minutes discussing center pieces. That's her job. Leave her to it. They will be beautiful.

- Don't micromanage. Just like in the case of your table decorations, once a woman on your team has volunteered to handle an aspect of the event or program, trust her with it. She may not do it exactly like you have in mind. She may do it better! God led you to make her part of your team. If you are doing someone else's job, you are not doing yours. Give her the freedom to use her gifts and her creativity in her role for God's glory. World War II General George Patton instructed leaders saying, "Never tell people how to do things. Tell them what you want them to do, and they will surprise you with their ingenuity."[1]

- Include personal moments at your meetings. Highlight gifts or talents or accomplishments you see in the women. Celebrate birthdays, listen to faith testimonies, thank them for a job well-done, and underscore faithfulness. Keep learning what motivates them and what discourages them. Notice what's going on in their personal lives and follow up. Dedicating ten meeting minutes to love and encourage the women on your team will prove invaluable.

HANDLING THE HARD PART

Regardless of how flawlessly you choose your team and lead your meetings, you will experience conflict. Volumes have been written about dealing with clashes and tensions between individuals and on teams. No advice has helped me more than the lessons taught in the book of Nehemiah.

God clearly directed and strengthened a group of Jewish exiles to returned to Jerusalem to rebuild its tumbledown wall . . . but not without significant conflict. Enemies of the Jews, sponsored by the evil one, tried varied means of discouraging and thwarting all their wall building efforts. God's appointed leader, Nehemiah, prayed, and addressed his "team," creatively providing them means of defending themselves while never stopping their God-ordained work (Neh. 4, 6). Interesting enough, sandwiched in between the intense conflict with their enemies in chapters 4 and 6, Nehemiah's team faced internal discord (Neh. 5). We can glean two important truths from his dealings with team tension:

> 1. Face team conflict. Unlike the conflict from "without," which provided greater motivation, unity, and served to move the project forward, Nehemiah handled the conflict "within" quite differently. External conflict spurred them on to continuing their labors. As soon as he heard about the internal disputes, however, Nehemiah pushed pause on their

work, listened to the grievances, brought the people together, and dealt with the problem in short order (Neh. 5:1–8). He made it clear that the people of God are to live in ways that bring glory to him, showing their detractors his greatness (Neh. 5:9). Their selfish behavior and thoughtless treatment of their fellow countrymen was doing just the opposite.

Like the Jewish wall builders, women's ministry teams are made up of diverse, image-bearing, yet sinful individuals. We each have our own ideas and strong opinions. We sometimes operate out of immaturity or selfish motives. Fear of conflict can drive leaders to choose sides, retreat to secretive backroom whisperings, or cross their fingers in hopes that it will all go away. It doesn't go away. As one theologian so aptly put it, "Sin is both fatal and fertile."[2]

We must see sinful disputes and tensions as the unity destroyers they are and deal with them head on, immediately. Bringing about face-to-face dialogue, clarification of issues, and rightful restoration can draw to a close what will otherwise fester.

2. Embrace team conflict. Although anything but enjoyable, we can embrace conflict among team members as a God-given occasion for refining one another and improving outcomes. Nehemiah didn't just listen to the issues raised, he gave clear instructions as to how to move forward and correct the wrongs. He obtained a promise of restitution from the guilty party, restored hope for those hurt, and continued to model for all generous, godly behavior.

God teaches us that "iron sharpens iron, and one person sharpens another" (Prov. 27:17). As iron is being sharpened, sparks fly. See the process through because the outcome is worth it. Get those together who are at odds. Encourage truth-speaking with love. Separate the problem from the person and work the problem. A well-handled conflict can often result in stronger relationships, better ideas, and a godly pattern for dealing with future issues that will inevitably arise.

You are creating a leadership culture by the way you lead and build a team. You are modeling best practices for all the hearts and stars God has put in your care. They are learning from you how to love others and how to lead others. As a leader in ministries to women, your role is not that of an event coordinator, although you may do that. It is not that of a program designer and implementor, although you may do that as well. Neither is it that of a meeting chairperson, although you'll certainly do that. You are shepherding women. Those women must know that you care about their hearts and that you are committed to their development as stars for the glory of God.

REVIEW AND DISCUSS

1. Teamwork can be challenging and cumbersome! What difficulties have you encountered in working with a team? Going forward, what strategies in recruiting women would you use to help overcome these obstacles?

2. In choosing a team, what various criteria are important to consider? What value do you see in writing out a job description? What would you include in that description?

3. When recruiting, why is focusing on the personal qualities which the role requires a better approach than emphasizing the position/title you are filling? How might it improve your ability to find the right person?

4. What have you learned from Nehemiah about dealing with conflict? What are some of the potentially positive results of a well-handled conflict?

CHAPTER 10

Growing and Leading Faithfully

FROM EARLY ON IN my Christian life, I believed that I was supposed to have one person who would disciple me. Without that one, godly woman who would lead the way in loving, teaching, and correcting me to spiritual maturity, I would be short-changed and would lag behind in growing as a believer. But God's call on my husband's and my life moved us to various locations, including overseas, often with the job of reaching and discipling younger believers than ourselves. So instead of that one woman to walk alongside me, what I experienced was somewhat of a mishmash: a person here, a sermon there, an influential book, a timely podcast, a significant conference, and the impactful words of a friend. Years later, an elder at our church used a diagram to describe what growth in the Christian life most often looks like—and what it doesn't.[1] Here's what it DOESN'T look like:

Yes, as a Christian, our journey to maturity involves a growing relationship between the teacher/discipler and the learner/disciple. It requires someone to model what they're teaching and to guide us through new and varied experiences. It involves correction and redirection, encouragement and support. But our discipler will most likely not be one older friend who commits to walking with us throughout our lives. Our one true discipler is Jesus. Jesus uses his Spirit, his Word, his people, (including pastors, podcasters, authors, conference speakers, and friends), and his ordained circumstances to get us where he wants us to be: not perfect, but more like him than when we started. And he uses these things in the order that is best for each of us as individuals. There's no universal starting point of growth once you've placed your faith in Jesus. There's no absolute right (or wrong) sequence to his syllabus. And there's no "final lesson" in his curriculum. As we travel down the river of growth towards maturity in Christ, we will be offered what we need as we need it through the various means that he supplies. It is our privilege and responsibility to look to Jesus, trust him to provide it, and take advantage of what he puts in our paths. Our growth journey looks much more like this:

Starting point as a new believer

Lake of spiritual maturity

How this frees us up as teachers, mentors, and guides of others! Yes, we pray about how we should be leading women. Yes, we think about how to order our teaching or mentoring so as to lay solid foundations, build upon them, and not overwhelm and discourage newer believers with unrealistic expectations. Yes, we ask God to show us how to stretch ourselves so that we can challenge more mature believers to go deeper. But God ordains their growth and ours. Wherever we live, whoever we know, whatever circumstances in which we find ourselves, God will provide avenues for growth. He will "line the banks" of the meandering river toward our maturity and the maturity of all those we lead with everything necessary.

I am sure of this, that he who started a good
work in you will carry it on to completion
until the day of Christ Jesus. (Phil. 1:6)

God's Word illustrates this riverbank reality for us in an unusual way. Moses is known for his leadership of God's people through their miraculous escape from slavery under Egypt's cruel Pharaoh. But this epic account in the book of Exodus doesn't begin with God grabbing Moses's attention at the burning bush or his appointment of him as the leader. It begins instead with the details of how God used five different women to make the rest of the story possible. These women demonstrated enormous courage and faith, used the abilities and positions granted to them, and trusted God with the consequences.

In Exodus 1, we meet Shiphrah and Puah, Egyptian midwives, who in bold defiance of the pharaoh's decree, didn't kill the male children (including Moses) born to the Hebrew women. We see Moses's mother, hiding her son for three months, then heart-wrenchingly giving him up with the desire to save his life. We are introduced to Moses's sister, Miriam, who watches over him as he floats in his basket in the

Nile. Pharaoh's daughter, knowing the baby was a condemned Hebrew child, after discovering him, took him from the basket and adopted him as her own. Miriam then daringly spoke up to this powerful woman and offered to find a nurse—Moses's own mother—for the child (Exod. 1:15–2:10).

Five women, different in upbringing, ethnicity, status, and calling, were used by God to spare and shape the life of a leader of his people. Each played her unique, vital role. Each trusted God, unsure of the outcome.

Throughout Moses's life, he had to learn from God, step-by-step, through prayer, people, and experiences. He wasn't understudy to a discipler who could provide all the answers or explain the best way forward. We can only guess what upbringing he received from his adoptive mother and what teaching he obtained in Pharaoh's court. After Moses was enlisted as the leader of his people, God not only taught him face to face, but also brought in others to advise and redirect him. He used Moses's wife, Zipporah, to save his life by carrying out an act of obedience Moses had left undone (Exod. 4:24–26). And Moses's father-in-law had to advise him regarding how to delegate responsibility so as not to wear himself out and frustrate the people (Exod. 18:13–27).

We have no idea the effect of our decisions or actions or investments in other's lives. Some piece of advice or courageous act may have a life-altering impact. What we do know is that God has made us in his image and as such we are to lead others to grow to know him, become more like him, and spread his fame. Hannah Anderson writes, "the fact that women are made to lead isn't up for debate. Made in God's image, we were not made to be passive any more than he is. We are actors. We are agents. We are makers. We are leaders."[2]

Whether or not you have a title or a job description, you are a leader. Women lead as mothers, as neighbors, as professionals, as coworkers, and as friends. Some of you will be tapped on the shoulder when you least expect it to lead as women's directors in your church.

That's what happened to me.

One otherwise uneventful day, I received a call from my pastor asking to meet. A few days later, he laid out for me the need for a director of the women's ministry at our church. Previously led by various volunteers, he wanted to establish a recognized position with the goal of helping women grow and having their well-being represented at the staff meetings. As he explained the role to me, my response to his job offer changed from excitement to hesitancy to downright fear. I loved the idea, but our church was an historic one with many spiritually mature women. My previous ministry experience was with a parachurch organization, and my current "ministry experience" was raising three kids and presently homeschooling my youngest. I didn't know the "ropes" of church ministry and failure flashed before my eyes! So finally I said to him, "This sounds like a great opportunity, but I'm not confident that I'm the right person. There are women in this church who have been walking with God a lot longer than I have. Many are wiser than I am. And some have much more experience than I do." Now I know the response that I hoped for and that I honestly anticipated receiving. Something like, "Oh no, but you have a strong walk with God. Others have witnessed your wisdom. And your ministry experience is just what I am looking for!" But he didn't say any of that. What he said instead was, "That's probably true. But if God is calling you to lead in this way, you need to lead. You should pray about it."

Oh, I prayed. And God led me to a passage of Scripture which left no doubt in my mind that he personally directs his children. The verses I read explained God's choosing of David to be king, the experience that prepared him for that role, and the assets necessary to carry it out. The end of Psalm 78 reads like this:

> [God] chose David his servant
> and took him from the sheep pens;
> he brought him from tending ewes
> to be shepherd over his people Jacob—
> over Israel, his inheritance.
> He shepherded them with a pure heart
> and guided them with his skillful hands.
> (Ps. 78:70–72)

The role I was being asked to consider was certainly not a royal one! But what this passage showed me was that 1) God does the choosing from unexpected places, 2) tending ewes (and some translations say "lambs") could indeed be preparation to shepherd people, and 3) what David needed for his new job was a pure heart and skillful hands. God saw David in the sheep pens and eventually transferred him to a palace. He wasn't chosen by God to be king because he had previous kingly experience. His skills in shepherding were the asset God wanted to use in this new role. And what mattered to God in choosing a shepherd of his people was the purity of David's heart and the skillfulness of his hands.

I recognized the truth in what my pastor had said. God does the choosing—even from seemingly unlikely places. And I knew that I had prioritized my little lambs and was doing my best at shepherding them well. I had a ways to go in the purity of my heart and the skills necessary for the job. But I was committed to trusting God with those as I grew to know him better, become more like him, and make him famous.

God has chosen you for a role in his kingdom. It may be that at this point in time only he knows what that looks like. You can be certain that whatever the role, he sees you right where you are, he is preparing you for it, and wants to cultivate in you a pure heart and skillful hands.

As opportunities open up for you, seek God and barring any red flags, step into them. We can easily find excuses to stay in the sheep pens, but what we miss if we do!

I often revisit Jesus's words to his disciples as I think about my ministry and encourage women in theirs. Jesus gave the disciples great authority, specific instructions, and dire warnings. He made sure they knew that even as they operated in the center of God's will, they would have difficult days and anxiety-producing encounters (Matt. 10:17–23). So will we. He commanded them to fear God, and nothing or no one else. So should we. God is the one who numbers every hair we have on our heads and counts every sparrow that falls to the ground (Matt. 10:26–31). He knows everything, loves us perfectly, and is our infinitely faithful caregiver. The better we know him, the greater our awe, respect, and trust of him grows. We can no longer find any excuse to fear failure or hold back from doing his will. We can step out in faith and embrace the absolute truth that he is shaping us into his likeness.

Jesus made sure to include in his instructions that his disciples be "as shrewd as serpents and as innocent as doves" (Matt. 10:16). So must we. To be shrewd means to be clever or wise in practical matters. Nothing is more practical than having a growing knowledge of the God who made us, learning from him in all our circumstances. To be innocent means we are free from guilt or wrongdoing. That freedom comes graciously from God alone, through Christ's purchase of our forgiveness on the cross. It is that gospel innocence that will help shape us more and more into Christ's likeness and enable us to spread his fame.

We have seen together how vital it is, not only for women, but for all of God's church that we provide teaching, training, and ministry opportunities for all the females in our midst. Whether we are reaching out to a few or to an entire megachurch of women, we need to know where to start. We begin with these God-ordained ends in mind: knowing God as he is, becoming more like him, and making him famous. All that we do should contribute to reaching these ends.

In order to move forward in attaining God's desired outcomes, we must start right where we are. Ambitious plans and a huge vision might be exciting, but God has intentionally made us limited beings and placed us in a limited world. What we have is just what we need to pursue God's goals for us.

Throughout this book, you have found ideas and examples of possible ways to reach God's desired ends in discipling women. You have been alerted to the dangers of putting programs ahead of people and urged over and over again to keep your ministry personal and relational. Knowing the women you are discipling and the context in which you are serving are indispensable elements to guide you along the way.

As God so amply illustrates in his Word, he cares little for outward appearances when choosing his servants, but majors in heart attitudes. We should do the same as we choose ministry leaders. We are not looking for glitzy stars but are definitely in search of humble hearts. And those hearts will come in a vast array of different packages—socio-economically, racially, stages of life, personalities, interests, and giftings. As we are selecting leaders, we pray for eyes to see what God sees, take the time needed to listen to his voice, and follow his lead. We always keep in mind that none of us has arrived, so potential-seeking is essential!

Having been directed by God to potential leaders, helping them to realize that potential starts with us. We are the examples—flawed as we are. We encourage growth in others by walking with God ourselves and pointing them to him in our successes and our failures. Then we take the initiative to institute vital steps we often omit in ministries to women: we provide practical training, hands-on opportunities, give feedback for improvement, and follow that with more hands-on opportunities. Putting the development of others first—polishing God's chosen stars—will have sure and lasting kingdom consequences.

Working hard to help women grow to spiritual maturity is fulfilling and admirable. Believing that it all depends on us is not. We looked at God's instructions to us to remember him: That he is in control. That all we are and all we have are from him. That he loves us, provides for us, and remains forever faithful to us. Forgetfulness regarding who God is, what he has done, and what he is doing is destructive for our walk with him and devastating to our ministry. We are commanded by God to establish means of remembering and take times to rest. Resting demonstrates in a tangible way our trust in the fact that God can run the universe without our help. We set an example for ourselves and for those around us by instituting rhythms of work and rest in both our personal lives and our ministries.

Last, we looked together at the ins and outs of teamwork. We discussed how to form effective ministry teams by finding the right people and putting them in the right places. Recognizing that groups of women are organic and not static, we focused on keeping them healthy through intentional planning, providing personal attention, and diligently dealing with disputes.

Living our lives in order to:

- know God as he is and help others know him,
- become like God and help others grow into his likeness, and
- spread God's fame and encourage that fame-spreading in others,

is an unmatched privilege which is beautifully afforded to each of us. It is essential then that we teach, train, mentor, and cultivate opportunities for women to flourish for the glory of God and the building up of his church. Women's maturity as believers must matter to us because it matters so much to God. And God chooses imperfect, image-bearing, faithful women like you to make it happen.

REVIEW AND DISCUSS

1. As you think back on your spiritual journey up to this point, take some time to name pivotal people, circumstances, books, and/or teachings that God has placed in your path to help you grow. Do you believe that he will continue to supply all the avenues of growth you need?

2. Are you convinced that God sees you and has chosen you for a role in his kingdom? Do you see yourself as someone God may use to impact another's life towards spiritual maturity? How can you live now ready for the opportunities God will open up for you?

3. Fear of failure can thwart our willingness to step into ministry occasions God has for us. What truths about God help you overcome fears and step out in faith?

4. Knowing God as he is, becoming more like him, and making him famous are the goals that God has for us. How are you prioritizing your life's choices to reach these goals? How are you teaching, training, mentoring, and cultivating opportunities for other women to flourish for the glory of God and the building up of his church?

Guidelines for Structuring a Discipleship School

Discipleship School is a course to help believers mature in their faith through the teaching and application of foundational Christian doctrines and practices.

DEVELOP YOUR CURRICULUM

Choose a theology book[1] to help structure and inform your doctrinal study, then select the chapter topics to cover, and assign a date to each. Order them in a way that builds knowledge from the "ground up" and best suits the needs of your participants. Also include lessons on spiritual formation practices and their "how-tos."

Beginning with "Sharing our faith stories" will help you discern women's gospel understanding and their spiritual maturity as they verbalize their conversion testimony.

Depending on your group and the time frame of your "school," you may want to give more teaching and application space to some topics over others or rearrange the order in which you teach them. There is freedom and flexibility!

If available, invite those trained in theology to teach doctrinal lessons, or instead, study together using one of the suggested books. (See "Resources" at the end of this Appendix.)

Suggested Topics

Sharing our faith stories

Discipleship

God and his attributes

The life and work of Jesus

The gospel

The Scriptures

Bible study methods, memorization, and meditation

Prayer

Women's identity

The Holy Spirit

The church

Serving in the local church

The Trinity

The mission of God

As topics are covered, include application. For example, what difference does it make in our lives that God is good, wise, and sovereign? Or that the Word of God is living and active? Or that we are children of God by faith and not by works? Or that the church is described as a family?

Homework may include reading the assigned chapter and/or an online article, studying a Bible passage, and memorizing a relevant verse.

Make sure to give the participants real-life experiences in discipling others. It's essential! Provide instruction and a guide so that each can help another grow in her knowledge of God, her spreading of his fame, and her Christlikeness. A sample guide follows.

SCRIPTURAL GUIDE FOR DISCIPLESHIP—8 SESSIONS

1. Share Your Faith Stories with One Another

As your disciples share, listen for a clear understanding of who Christ is, what he did, and how his death in our place and resurrection impact their lives in an ongoing way. Do they understand that they *didn't* and *can't* earn salvation? Do they trust in Christ's work on their behalf? Ephesians 2:1–10 explains this beautifully!

You can use the following outline to talk about your stories:

- Describe your life before you knew Christ as God and Savior.
- How did you come to know him?
- What difference does knowing Christ make in your life?
- How would you describe him to someone else?

First Peter 3:15–16 and Colossians 4:2–6 help explain the importance of *how* we share our stories.

2. God's Word

Read each passage and *discuss together* what it teaches us *about God* and *about his Word*.

   2 Tim. 3:16–17

   Deut. 32:46–47

   1 Peter 1:22–25

   Matt. 4:4

   Isa. 55:10–11

   Heb. 4:12–13

How should we live in light of these truths?

Talk about what a daily "quiet time" or "time alone with God" might look like: What's the purpose of it? What do you do? Where do you start? What do you read?

3. Jesus Christ

1. What is true about Jesus according to the passages below? What about Jesus surprises or confuses you? Is attractive to you?
2. What aspect of your life would you like to see conformed to *this* Jesus?
3. Record one truth that you want to remember about Jesus from these passages.

> Isa. 53:1–12
>
> John 13:1–15
>
> Matt. 9:1–13
>
> John 14:1–7
>
> John 1:1–18
>
> Phil. 2:5–11

4. The Gospel

The gospel is the good news that we enter God's kingdom through God's cross by God's grace. Look carefully at the passages below.

1. What truth does the gospel contain about Jesus? About us?
2. What impact does the gospel have on us who believe it?
3. How can the gospel affect our thinking and behavior in hard times? When we sin?

1 Cor. 15:1–6

Titus 3:3–8

2 Cor. 5:16–21

Col. 1:15–23

5. Grace

Grace is God's acceptance of us not because we have earned it or deserved it but because he gives it to us freely at Christ's expense. According to the verses below . . .

> 1. How do we acquire grace? What is God's role? What is our role?
> 2. What does it look like to live in grace?
> 3. What are the enemies of God's grace in our life? How do we overcome them?

> > Eph. 1:3–14
> >
> > Rom. 6:1–14
> >
> > Eph. 2:1–10
> >
> > 2 Tim. 1:8–10
> >
> > Rom. 5:12–21
> >
> > 2 Cor. 12:9–10

6. The Holy Spirit

Read the following passages and answer the questions to come to a broader and deeper understanding of the Holy Spirit. Each passage won't answer all the questions, but together they will help you grow in your knowledge of the Spirit and how you are to relate to him.

1. Who is the Holy Spirit? What other names describe him and how do they help our understanding of him?

2. How is the Holy Spirit at work in our lives? What does he do?

3. What is living by the flesh vs. living by the Spirit? How are you living?

> John 3:1–8
>
> Rom. 8:1–17, 26–27; Eph. 5:15–21
>
> John 14:15–17, 25–26
>
> 1 Cor. 12:1–13
>
> John 16:4–15
>
> Gal. 5:16–26

7. The Church

The church is the people that God has made alive, called together, and sent on mission. It is God's family of worshippers, servants, disciples, and witnesses.

1. According to the passages below, what are some of the characteristics of God's church? Describe it.
2. What are the purposes of the church?
3. How does being a part of God's church impact you?

> Acts 2:42–47
>
> Eph. 2:13–22; 4:11–16
>
> Col. 3:12–17
>
> 1 Pet. 2:9–12

8. Spiritual Growth

Growth is a lifelong partnership with the Holy Spirit to change and become like Jesus. The Holy Spirit uses his Word, prayer, people, and trials to transform us.

As you read through the following passages, take note of what God uses to change us and what attitudes and actions on our part contribute to our growth as Christians.

> Ps. 1:1–3
>
> Phil. 1:27–30; 4:4–7
>
> 1 Cor. 10:13
>
> 2 Tim. 3:16–17
>
> Gal. 5:22–26
>
> James 1:22–25
>
> Heb. 12:3–13
>
> Phil. 2:12–16

RESOURCES

Nothing grows our relationship with God like time spent with him and his church, in his Word and in prayer. The books listed below are good resources to help you know God through his Word and challenge you to deepen your understanding of life with God.

50 Core Truths by Gregg Allison

Bible Doctrine by Wayne Grudem

Everyday Theology: What You Believe Matters by Mary Wiley

Gentle and Lowly by Dane Ortlund

In His Image by Jen Wilkin

Life's Biggest Questions by Eric Thoennes

Made for More by Hannah Anderson

None Like Him by Jen Wilkin

Women of the Word by Jen Wilkin

Word-Filled Women's Ministry by Gloria Furman and Kathleen Nielson

You Are a Theologian by Jen Wilkin and J. T. English

Training Group Facilitators

(Adapted from group leader training designed by Terri Derhake)

*As you train women to lead small groups, including
the following information verbally and in writing
will keep your ministry goal in mind and provide
guidance to your leaders.*

1. Vision: Remind women of the "why" of the particular ministry so she knows what her small group is intended to accomplish. A group for mentoring will differ from a cohort centered on doctrine, and a Bible study discussion group's purpose is not the same as one designed for prayer. Is your primary goal for the women in the groups to know God better through the study of his Word, or is it to grow in intimacy with God through honesty and humility in their prayer life? Focusing on the group's goal will free the facilitator from trying to "do it all" and aid greatly in her sense of successfully carrying out her role.

2. Character: Reiterate the Christlike characteristics God desires and is working to develop in us. You can use God's words through Micah: "He has told each of you what is good and what it is the LORD requires of you: to act justly, to love faithfulness, and to walk humbly with your God" (Mic. 6:8). This is also displayed in Paul's exhortation on the fruit of the Holy Spirit (Gal. 5:22–23). Remind all your group leaders why you asked them to step into this role and that their walk with God is primary.

3. Responsibilities: In training, spell out the expectations of a group leader.

- How much time do you anticipate she will need to spend per week/per month? Outside of the meeting time, do you envision her praying for her group members? Or reaching out to each via text, email, or in person?
- If you expect her to "care for" or "disciple" the women in her group, explain

what that means. For example: Disciple each woman in your group by praying for her, reaching out to her, and when appropriate, diagnosing problems and pointing her to extra resources—all for the purpose of seeing her become more like Jesus and better equipped to disciple others.

- What is her role during the group time? As a facilitator and not a teacher, give her an idea of how she is to guide the discussion—and perhaps the percentage of time she should talk compared with women in her group.

- What is she listening for and directing toward in the discussion? During a Women's Discipleship School cohort, for example, she is trying to assess each woman's understanding, application, and her ability to articulate the truth being studied. In a Bible study, she is looking for the character of God, gospel truths, and heart change.

- Explain other requirements you may have for this role, for example, membership in your church and commitment to your church's vision.

4. Training: Provide facilitators with ample input to enable them to have a positive experience.

Address questions like:

- How do we want women in your group to feel? (Accepted, welcomed, cared for)
- What do we want women to know and understand? (God's ways, works, and will; how to walk with him; the gospel and its implications in all of life; how to study and apply God's Word)
- How can you ask good questions to enable and not dominate the discussion? (open-ended)
- When should you step in to correct wrong ideas and how should you do it

so as not to offend individual members of the group?

5. Handling Group Dynamics: How to deal with a group member who dominates the discussion:

- We don't want a woman to feel shut off, but at the same time, the responsibility of facilitators is to encourage discussion by all the women. Make sure the woman is heard, then try to shift the discussion to someone else. Here are some suggestions:

  "That's great____, maybe you could talk to me about that more later.
  Anyone else?"

- A coleader could help by summarizing something the "talker" said, then contributing her own thought to the discussion.
- Go back to the text/topic of discussion.
- Saying: "I'd love to hear more about that when we're done, but I want to make sure we have time for others to share on

this topic right now." Or, "This is an interesting question. Thanks for getting us going on it. What do the rest of you think?"

- Outside of the group time, ask her to help you in getting the others to participate. Explain that you are going to allow silence to help the quieter women feel comfortable speaking. She could watch you during silence to see when you want her to come in with her answer. (Her answer is very important, but she is waiting to give it.)

- Give her grace. Seek to make her feel heard and understood by talking with her before and/or after the discussion time.

How to deal with a quiet group member:

- Create space with silence. Explain to the group that a bit of silence helps everyone think about the question. "Let's ponder this for a moment."

- Ask her to read a small section of the text.
- Be aware of her body language. If she seems like she wants to jump in, but others are talking, you could say, "_____ did you have something you wanted to add? It looked like you were getting ready to talk."
- "What do the rest of you think? Is there anyone who hasn't had a chance to talk yet that wants to contribute to this question?"
- Give her grace. Seek to make her feel heard and understood by making sure to talk with her before and after the discussion time. She may be someone who doesn't talk for any number of reasons.

When and how to redirect a rabbit trail:

- Not all tangents are bad. Sometimes a quick rabbit trail can be beneficial for a group. *A tangent can cover material related to the subject that isn't going to be covered by a specific question but is on the minds of everyone in your group.* In this case, take a moment to address the issue, and then get back on track.

- Sometimes a group may need a tangent to get everyone talking. Groups can feel dull if no one is participating, and occasionally a quick rabbit trail may engage everyone and get them ready to talk about the main subject. And remember, the Holy Spirit may be doing something! If the direction of the conversation is taking you to a place where the women are talking about how God is working in their lives or where they feel challenged to take new steps of faith, then let it go for a bit.

- *As the leader you need to be the one to bring the group back to the guide.* This is an important part of group leadership. Group members get frustrated when tangents go on too long. In a light-hearted way you can say something like:

    "Okay, that was an interesting (and it might even have been important) 'rabbit trail,' but now let's get back to our questions." You can use a gesture, such as using both hands to create a "T" where you say, "Time out! Okay, back to question 4 (or wherever things got off track)."

- One of the best ways to get back on track is to tie the tangent back to the main point.

6. Inform your group facilitators of what they can expect from you. Things like:

- We will pray for you and meet with you regularly to help you grow in your knowledge of God and as a discipler of women.
- We will provide you with additional resources you may need for your formation and to help you serve the women in your group.

Devotional Questions: 70 Days with God in His Word

Each day, read the designated passage, ask the questions supplied, and write your thoughts in a journal.

GETTING TO KNOW JESUS

Day 1: Matthew 9:1–13	Day 8: John 7:10–24
Day 2: Mark 4:35–41	Day 9: John 7:25–36
Day 3: Matthew 8:1–4	Day 10: John 7:37–44
Day 4: John 8:1–11	Day 11: John 12:44–50
Day 5: Luke 24:13–27	Day 12: John 13:1–15
Day 6: John 1:43–51	Day 13: John 14:1–7
Day 7: John 4:46–54	Day 14: John 14:8–21

1. What characteristic(s) of Jesus do you find in this passage?
2. What about Jesus surprises or confuses you?
3. What question(s) would you like to ask Jesus? (Ask him now!)
4. What is the response to Jesus by those in this passage? What is your response?
5. What aspect of your life would you like to see conformed to this Jesus?
6. Record one truth that you want to remember from this passage.

GOING DEEPER

1. Read the passage in context (the verses before and after the selected passage). What further insight does this provide?

2. What is the main point of this passage? Write it in a short phrase or sentence.

3. Record any commands to follow, sins to avoid, promises to embrace.

4. Using cross references found in the margins of your Bible, see if the same account is recorded in another Gospel or portion of Scripture. How does this deepen your understanding?

GETTING TO KNOW GOD THE FATHER

Day 15: Jeremiah 9:23–24	Day 22: Psalm 32:1–11
Day 16: 1 Chron. 16:23–36	Day 23: Titus 3:3–7
Day 17: Job 38:1–16	Day 24: Psalm 78:34–39
Day 18: Micah 6:6–8	Day 25: Psalm 139:7–12
Day 19: Isaiah 1:10–20	Day 26: Psalm 139:13–18
Day 20: Isaiah 45:1–7	Day 27: Psalm 145:14–21
Day 21: Psalm 23:1–6	Day 28: Jeremiah 32:36–42

What is true about God according to this passage? Don't miss anything!

1. How do these truths about God change the way you view him? Your present circumstances? The way you pray?

2. What types of actions/responses most please God? Most displease him?

3. What, if anything, about God's character makes you uncomfortable? Talk to him about it.

4. What would you like to ask God to change in your life in order to be more like him?

5. Record one truth you want to take away from this passage.

GOING DEEPER

1. Discover the "big picture" from which this passage was taken. What are the circumstances? Who are the people?

2. Compare and contrast two or more of this section's passages. Put together a composite of the character of God revealed in these verses.

3. Which of God's characteristics are his alone? Which can we emulate?

4. Read all of Job 38 and 39 through 40:2. How would you answer God's questions?

5. Write a prayer of praise to God incorporating his revealed character.

GROWING IN YOUR WALK WITH GOD'S SPIRIT

Day 29: John 14:25–26	Day 36: Psalm 139:7–18
Day 30: 1 Cor. 2:6–16	Day 37: John 16:5–15
Day 31: Romans 8:1–11	Day 38: Ephesians 1:11–14
Day 32: Romans 8:12–17	Day 39: 1 Cor. 12:1–11
Day 33: Romans 8:18–30	Day 40: 1 Cor. 6:9–11
Day 34: Ephesians 5:15–21	Day 41: Acts 2:1–13
Day 35: Galatians 5:16–26	Day 42: Acts 2:14–21

1. If you had to introduce the Holy Spirit to a friend, what would you say using this passage?

2. What "work" does the Holy Spirit do in peoples' lives? Do you experience this in your life?

3. Reflect on various aspects of your life (relationships, church involvement,

work, and so forth). What difference would you expect to see if you were totally yielded to the Holy Spirit in each area?

4. Pray now for God's Spirit to work more freely and powerfully in a particular area of your life this week. Record your prayer and what changes you see.

GOING DEEPER

Using a concordance, do a word study on the Holy Spirit (and God's Spirit, the Spirit) making a list of his activities recorded in Scripture. What personal insights does this provide into his possible and desired involvement in your life?

GROWING IN PRAYER

Day 43: Matthew 6:5–8	Day 50: Psalm 40:16–17
Day 44: Matthew 6:9–15	Day 51: Psalm 27:1–14
Day 45: Luke 11:5–10	Day 52: Psalm 63:1–8
Day 46: John 15:4–8	Day 53: Psalm 95:1–7

Day 47: Nehemiah 1:4–11	Day 54: Psalm 136:1–9
Day 48: Psalm 17:1–6	Day 55: Matthew 11:25–30
Day 49: Ephesians 3:14–21	Day 56: Ephesians 1:15–23

1. Write out a principle regarding prayer that is taught or exemplified in this passage.
2. What characteristic of God is discussed or appealed to in this passage?
3. What can you take from this passage to improve or enhance your prayer life?
4. Reflecting on his character, write out your own God-honoring, thoughtful prayer.

GOING DEEPER

1. If you have not already done so, set up a prayer system for yourself using a notebook or phone app to record prayer requests in various areas (personal, for friends and family, your church, governmental, missional, and so forth.). Pray for them regularly and record God's answers.

2. Plan a regular time to pray with a friend or family member. Praise God and bring him all your needs and hopes.

OBSERVING AND VALUING GOD'S WORD

Day 57: Psalm 1:1–3	Day 64: Psalm 119:1–8
Day 58: Psalm 19:7–14	Day 65: Psalm 119:17–24
Day 59: Psalm 33:4–9	Day 66: Psalm 119:33–40
Day 60: Nehemiah 8:1–12	Day 67: Psalm 119:41–48
Day 61: Nehemiah 8:13–18	Day 68: Psalm 119:97–104
Day 62: Deut. 6:1–9	Day 69: Psalm 119:105–112
Day 63: Deut. 6:20–25	Day 70: Psalm 119:137–144

1. Write down all the words used to name or describe God's Word.
2. What are the stated *results* of God's Word in the life of its hearers? What difference did it or will it make?
3. Write down the reactions or emotions generated by hearing God's Word in these passages. Are these ever your

reactions? If so, why and when? If not, why don't you think you react or feel similarly?

4. Choose one verse from this passage and observe it carefully. What do you see? Notice contrasts, repeated words, and cause-effect relationships. Define words. Note any people or places mentioned. What is the main verb in this verse? What tense is it? How does this verse fit into the paragraph or chapter?

5. Thank God for his Word and ask him to use it in your life to make you more like Christ.

GOING DEEPER

1. Return to the verse that you observed in question #4 and find at least ten additional observations that you missed.

2. Observe the whole section that you read today. Notice things that are:

- Emphasized
- Repeated
- Related
- Alike
- Unlike

Pay attention to the grammar: Are there commands? Statements? Questions? Conditional phrases ("if . . . then . . .")?

- Notice the adjectives, adverbs, subjects, and verbs.
- Without looking back at the passage, do you remember the big idea of what you read?

Know the Women, Know Your Church

KNOW THE WOMEN

1. What is her stage of life and background? (Married, single, children at home, working outside the home, from the area or a recent transplant, extended family in town?)

2. Invite her to talk about her spiritual journey. How would she describe her relationship with God? Her relationship to the church?

3. What are her biggest challenges at present? Does she have any specific prayer requests?

4. What are her hopes/desires regarding spiritual growth? What experiences, gifts, skills does she have that she would like to use?

KNOW YOUR CHURCH

1. Does your church have a written mission statement? If so, what is it? Will a ministry to and by women fit into the overall plan of your church?

2. What are the values and "personality" of your church?

3. What are women's current roles within your church?

4. Is your church urban, suburban, or country? What are the demographics? (Young or old? White or blue collar? Rich or poor?) Are new ministry ideas encouraged or looked at with suspicion? Do the leaders embrace change or find it disconcerting?

5. What is the structure of your church? Who might you approach with a new ministry idea and how? (A formal written proposal to a board? A casual conversation with a pastor or ministry leader?)

Mentor Training

*We proclaim him, warning and teaching
everyone with all wisdom,* so that we may
present everyone mature in Christ.
(Col. 1:28, emphasis added)

SPIRITUAL MENTORING

The primary function of a mentor is to provide guidance in a context of love and support so that spiritual growth may occur in another.

Who Can Mentor

1. Those who love God and his Word and walk with him in humility.

2. Those who understand the gospel and by the grace of God, are living it out.
3. Those who care about others' spiritual growth, are able to pass on spiritual truth, and will keep confidences.

Who to Invite to Be Mentored

1. Those who are teachable and desirous to learn.
2. Those who are willing to commit time and effort to their spiritual growth.
3. Those who respect others, both older and peers, and will keep confidences.

What a Mentor Does

1. Helps another grow to know God through his Word, trusts Jesus's work on the cross, and depends on his Spirit.

2. Helps another to notice God in her everyday life and then live accordingly. We remind women who God is, what he has done, and to live their lives in light of these truths.

3. Helps another see herself as God sees her. We hold up the "mirror" of God's Word so that women can see themselves as loved and chosen by God, and needy of him. We pass on wisdom, share lessons from our successes and failures, and help her love others authentically and sacrificially.

4. Helps another carry out her service in God's kingdom by identifying her gifts and abilities, encouraging her to use them skillfully and lovingly.

What Does Mentoring Look Like?

1. There is not one correct model. Small groups of two older mentors with three to six younger women enables the leaders to speak into younger women's lives while peer mentoring also takes place. Monthly times together, with "check-ins" by text or personal times in between is a good rhythm for many.

2. Time together can be spent:

   - in thankfulness and sharing "evidences of God" seen in women's lives

   - in God's Word and using the resources provided

   - looking for God's perspective in life's challenges

   - praying for one another

RESOURCES

Growing Together: Taking Mentoring Beyond Small Talk and Prayer Requests by Melissa B. Kruger

One-to-One Bible Reading: A Simple Guide for Every Christian by David Helm

Discipleship Essentials: A Guide to Building Your Life in Christ by Greg Ogden

Organic Mentoring: A Mentor's Guide to Relationships with Next Generation Women by Sue Edwards and Barbara Neumann

APPENDIX 6

Training Teachers

As you teach women to teach the Bible, help them learn:

- To identify the main idea and structure of a passage through thorough observation, careful interpretation, and gospel-centered application.
- To consider context of the passage: both the historical and literary.
- To interpret individual passages in light of the whole of Scripture and the obscure ideas in light of the clear.
- To not add to or subtract from the truth of the passage.

For a helpful list of questions to ask so that you might observe, interpret, and apply more productively, see bhpublishinggroup.com/AShortGuidetoWomensMinistry.

Give apprentice teachers the opportunity to:

- Study a passage of Scripture as you guide them through the process of observation, interpretation, and application.
- Outline the passage for themselves, giving them instruction and feedback.
- Fill in the details from the passage, learning what to omit and what to include.
- Work with examples, illustrations, and humor, teaching them the why, how, and when to use.
- Consider their audience and its needs.
- Prepare and deliver their own short teaching on a biblical passage, including an introduction, conclusion, and clarity in the passage's persuasive purpose. Give them praise and constructive feedback.

Provide questions for the apprentice teachers to ask themselves as they prepare:

1. What is the big idea that God is communicating in this text?

2. What truth about God's character is portrayed here?

3. How do I plan to substantiate the big idea and the truth of God's character from the text? (Look for sub-points in the text that support the big idea and what God is like.)

4. How do I plan to show the relevancy of this text to the women's lives? (Include illustrations, stories, and examples that make the points clear and relatable.)

5. Have I been thorough in doing my homework? (Have I prayed for the Spirit's insight, spent time in the text, defined any unclear words, searched cross references, understood the historical and

literary contexts, double-checked any theologically tricky ideas, and so forth?)

6. Have I considered the best way to communicate what God has taught me in this text? (Is there a fresh way to say this that will draw women in, help them better understand, relate, and stir their hearts toward God?)

EXAMPLE METHOD TO TRAIN TEACHERS: "JAMES IN 15"

With the goal of providing teaching opportunities for women to grow in their teaching skills, we divided the book of James into twelve sections (plus an introduction and a conclusion) and assigned each to apprentice teachers who had completed our in-person training. We asked each to prepare a teaching lasting fifteen minutes and use their phone to video their teaching.

We explained how to wisely use the time:

- Two minutes: Read and review the previous week's passage.

- Ten minutes: Remarks from the teacher (Explain and apply the passage).
- Three minutes: Respond (1–2 application questions, thoughts, prayer).

We worked with any teachers requesting help, and reviewed each one's lesson, providing feedback and encouragement before sharing it publicly to women in our church.

We provided a guide for the listeners as they heard the teaching like the following:

LISTENERS' GUIDE

Pray for the Holy Spirit to help you understand and apply this passage.

Read the passage three times, out loud if possible.

Ask these questions as you look at the Scripture passage:

1. What was the main idea in the previous passage? Does that shed light on this one?
2. What is the main idea of this passage?

3. Are there specific instructions, commands or promises in this text? Ponder these.

4. Is there something repeated or restated that God doesn't want me to miss? Are there any surprises here?

5. Are there any images or metaphors that James uses here? Pause and ask God what he is communicating through these.

6. What does this passage teach me about God? And knowing this to be true, how does it impact my perspective? What does this teach me about myself as his child? About life in my current circumstances?

7. In light of what James wanted his readers to know and to do, how is the Holy Spirit speaking to me?

An indispensable resource for training Bible study teachers is Charles Simeon Trust "First Principles" Women's Course. Its eight lessons guide learners step by step through how to study and teach for right understanding and application of a biblical text. (https://simeontrust.org/workshops/)

JAMES IN 15: FAITH THAT WORKS
PASSAGE BREAKDOWN

Passage
Introduction–James 1:1
James 1:2–18
James 1:19–27
James 2:1–13
James 2:14–26
James 3:1–12
James 3:13–18
James 4:1–12
James 4:13–17
James 5:1–6
James 5:7–12
James 5:13–20
Conclusion

The one who looks intently into the perfect law of freedom and perseveres in it, and is not a forgetful hearer but a doer who works—this person will be blessed in what he does.
—James 1:25

Notes

Chapter 1

1. Aristotle, *Generation of Animals: A Critical Guide*, ed. Andrea Falcon and David Lefebvre (Cambridge: Cambridge University Press, 2018).

2. Abigail Dodds, *(A)Typical Woman: Free, Whole, and Called in Christ* (Wheaton, IL: Crossway, 2019), 40, 62.

Chapter 2

1. James I. Packer, *Knowing God* (Downers Grove, IL: InterVarsity Press, 1973), 14–15.

2. Gregg Allison, *Baker Compact Dictionary of Theological Terms* (Grand Rapids: Baker Books, 2016), 187.

3. John Piper, "What Is God's Glory?" Desiring God, July 6, 2009, https://www.desiringgod.org/interviews/what-is-gods-glory--2.

Chapter 3

1. Erik Thoennes, *Life's Biggest Questions: What the Bible Says about the Things That Matter Most* (Wheaton, IL: Crossway, 2011).

2. Gregg R. Allison, *50 Core Truths of the Christian Faith: A Guide to Understanding and Teaching Theology* (Grand Rapids: Baker Books, 2018).

3. Wayne A. Grudem, *Bible Doctrine, Second Edition: Essential Teachings of the Christian Faith* (Grand Rapids: Zondervan Academic, 2022).

4. Mary Wiley, *Everyday Theology: What You Believe Matters* (Nashville: Lifeway Press, 2020).

5. Jen Wilkin and J. T. English, *You Are a Theologian: An Invitation to Know and Love God Well* (Brentwood, TN: B&H Publishing, 2023).

6. Donald S. Whitney, *Spiritual Disciplines for the Christian Life* (Colorado Springs: NavPress, 2002). John Ortberg, *The Life You've Always Wanted: Spiritual Disciplines for Ordinary People* (Grand Rapids: Zondervan, 2002). Richard J. Foster, *Celebration of Discipline: The Path to Spiritual Growth* (New York: HarperCollins, 2018). Mason King, *A Short Guide to Spiritual Disciplines: How to Become a Healthy Christian* (Nashville: B&H Publishing, 2023).

7. Jen Wilkin, *Women of the Word: How to Study the Bible with Both Our Hearts and Our Minds* (Wheaton, IL: Crossway, 2014). Kathleen Buswell Nielson, *Bible Study: Following the Ways of the Word* (Phillipsburg, NJ: P&R Publishing, 2011). Kay Arthur, *Lord, Teach Me to Study the Bible in 28 Days* (Eugene, OR: Harvest House Publishers, 2006/2008). David Helm, *One-to-One Bible Reading: A Simple Guide for Every Christian* (Kingsford, Australia: Matthias Media, 2011).

Chapter 6

1. Tara-Leigh Cobble, *The Bible Recap: A One-Year Guide to Reading and Understanding the Entire Bible* (Minneapolis: Bethany House, 2020), 77.

2. Bruce Boria, personal conversation.

Chapter 7

1. www.simeontrust.org; https://simeontrust.org/courses/first-principles-women/

Chapter 9

1. George S. Patton Jr., *War as I Knew It*, Chapter "Reflections and Suggestions" (Boston: Mariner Books, 1947/1995).

2. Cornelius Plantinga, Jr., *Not the Way It's Supposed to Be: A Breviary of Sin* (Grand Rapids: Wm. B. Eerdmans Publishing Co., 1995/1996).

Chapter 10

1. Diagram from Brad House, a church elder in a training for community group leaders.

2. Hannah Anderson, "Lead On: Thoughts on Women, Leadership, and Motherhood," January 29, 2015, https://www.sometimesalight.com/sometimes-a-light/1/post/2015/01/lead-thoughts-women-leadership-motherhood.html.

Appendix 1

1. Theology resources:

Gregg R. Allison, *50 Core Truths of the Christian Faith: A Guide to Understanding and Teaching Theology* (Baker Books, 2018).

Wayne A. Grudem, *Bible Doctrine, Second Edition: Essential Teachings of the Christian Faith* (Zondervan Academic, 2022).

Erik Thoennes, *Life's Biggest Questions: What the Bible Says about the Things That Matter Most* (Crossway, 2011).

Mary Wiley, *Everyday Theology: What You Believe Matters* (Lifeway Press, 2020).

Jen Wilkin and J. T. English, *You Are a Theologian: An Invitation to Know and Love God Well* (B&H Publishing, 2023).

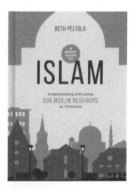
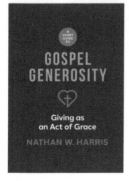
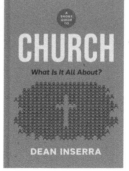